New Britain Common Council

The Charter and Ordinances of the City of New Britain

charter of the Water Works, and standing rules of the Common Council

New Britain Common Council

The Charter and Ordinances of the City of New Britain
charter of the Water Works, and standing rules of the Common Council

ISBN/EAN: 9783337300944

Printed in Europe, USA, Canada, Australia, Japan

Cover: Foto ©Andreas Hilbeck / pixelio.de

More available books at **www.hansebooks.com**

THE

CHARTER AND ORDINANCES

OF THE

CITY OF NEW BRITAIN,

CHARTER OF THE WATER WORKS,

AND ·

STANDING RULES OF THE COMMON COUNCIL.

Published by order of the Common Council, January, 1877.

———•••———

HARTFORD:
PRESS OF THE CASE, LOCKWOOD & BRAINARD COMPANY.
1877.

CHARTER

OF THE

CITY OF NEW BRITAIN,

ACCEPTED JANUARY 13, 1871,

AND AMENDMENTS.

AN ACT

INCORPORATING THE CITY OF NEW BRITAIN.

Be it enacted by the Senate and House of Representatives in General Assembly convened:

SECTION 1. All the inhabitants, being electors of this state, dwelling in the town of New Britain, within the following limits, to wit: commencing at a stone monument three hundred rods due west from the center of the front wall of the Normal School building in said town; thence running due north in a straight line two hundred and twelve rods to a stone monument; thence at right angles due east in a straight line six hundred rods to a stone monument; thence due south in a straight line parallel with said west line to the southerly limit of said town, at a stone monument; thence westerly on said southerly limit of said town to a stone monument; thence due north in a straight line parallel with said east line to place of beginning, being the community hitherto incorporated and known under the name of the warden, burgesses and freemen of the borough of New Britain, are hereby constituted and declared to be and remain forever one and the same body politic and corporate, by the name of the city of New Britain; to have perpetual succession, to be one person in law, capable of suing and being sued, pleading and being impleaded in all suits whatsoever, and of purchasing, holding and conveying any estate, real and personal, to have a common seal, with power to change the same, and to hold and exercise such powers and privileges hitherto exercised by said borough as are perpetuated herein, together with all the additional powers and privileges herein and hereby conferred.

SEC. 2. The city shall be divided into three* wards designated and bounded as follows, to wit: The first ward shall embrace all inhabitants and territory south of a line commencing at the western limit of said city, and running due east to the center of the west end of Walnut street, thence along the center line of Walnut street, to Main street; thence along the center line of said Main street to Park street; thence along the center line of said Park street to the east end thereof; thence due east to the eastern limit of said city. The second ward shall embrace all inhabitants and territory between the first and third wards. The third ward shall embrace all the inhabitants and territory north of a line commencing on the western limit of said city, and running thence due east to the center of the west end of Lafayette street; thence on the center line

---

* Altered to four by amendment of June 17, 1874.

of Lafayette street to Main street; thence on the center line of Main street to East Main street; thence on the center line of East Main street to the east end thereof; thence due east to the eastern limit of said city.

Sec. 3. Every elector of this state who shall have statedly and continuously resided in said city six months, shall thereafter, while such residence continues, and while his name is registered as hereinafter provided, be entitled to vote at all meetings of said city, and all meetings of the ward in which he may reside : *Provided*, that wherever any such voter shall have changed his residence from one ward into another during the thirty days preceding a meeting for the election of any officer or officers, he shall not be entitled to vote at such meeting in the latter ward, but shall be entitled to vote at such meeting in the former ward in the same manner as though he had not removed therefrom.

Sec. 4. An annual election shall be held by wards on the second Monday in April in each year, at which the voters of the city shall elect from their number by plurality of ballots, a mayor, a clerk, a treasurer, an auditor, a collector, and a sheriff for the city at large, and also one alderman, six* councilmen, and two inspectors of election for each of their respective wards; but no voter shall vote for more than one inspector of elections, and the two persons in each ward receiving the greatest number of ballots for the office of inspector of elections shall hold such offices as hereinafter provided. And the several aldermen shall take rank and precedence according to the number of ballots they may have respectively received for said office, and the alderman who has received the highest number of ballots shall be denominated first alderman, and the others shall be denominated second and third, according to the number of ballots by them respectively received; and in case two or more aldermen shall have received an equal number of ballots then the common council of said city shall, at their first meeting determine, by ballot, the rank and precedence of such alderman. All officers elected by the city at large shall be residents of said city, and all officers elected by the several wards shall be residents of such wards, and shall vacate their offices by removal therefrom. All officers elected at such annual election shall hold office for the term of one year, commencing at noon of the third Monday of April following, and until their successors are elected and .qualified.

---

* Altered to four by amendment of June 17, 1874.

SEC. 5.   Wherever at any such meeting there shall be no election to an office by reason of a tie vote, then said meeting shall stand adjourned to the next following Monday, at the same hour as when first held, and the election to fill such office shall be proceeded with in the same manner and upon the same registry list as on said first day.   Whenever a vacancy shall occur in any of the offices named in the preceding section, the common council shall order a special election to be held within two weeks thereafter at which a successor shall be elected to fill such vacancy, at which special election the same body of electors only shall be entitled to vote, by which the office was conferred upon him whose successor is so to be elected.

SEC. 6.   The registrars of voters of the town of New Britain in making out the lists now required by law to be made by them. shall designate opposite the names of the electors of said town, residing in said city, the ward in which each elector resides; and it shall be the duty of said registrars to prepare from such registry lists, separate alphabetical lists, authenticated by their signatures, of the electors in each ward. for the use of each inspector of elections of such ward : in performing which duty, said registrars shall simply transfer to such separate ward lists the names of electors that appear on the town list as residing in such wards ; such lists shall be prepared at the expense of said city, and shall be delivered to such inspectors before sunset of the day preceding the annual election.*

SEC. 7.   Every inspector of elections shall immediately upon taking his oath of office, appoint a deputy inspector, whose name and whose appointment shall be by him certified to the city clerk, and entered by him at the end of the record of the meeting at which such inspector was elected ; and such deputy may, in case of the absence or inability of the inspector, or whenever directed by the latter, perform all the duties of said inspector, and any inspector may, at any time, remove the deputy by him appointed and appoint another in his place, upon certifying the same to the city clerk, who shall record such change.

SEC. 8.   There shall be one place of voting in each ward at each election of officers, designated by the common council, who shall cause notice thereof to be published in a newspaper of said city, or in such manner as said common council by an ordinance

---

* Amended June 19, 1876.

shall prescribe, not more than four weeks nor less than two weeks preceding such election. The poll in each ward shall be open from nine o'clock in the forenoon until five o'clock in the afternoon, during every annual election, and at special elections during such time as the common council shall direct. The inspectors of elections of each ward shall designate from the voters of such ward, by agreement if possible, otherwise by lot, a presiding officer for election and assistants to relieve him in the duty of presiding; said inspectors shall be present personally or by deputy, with their voting lists prepared as hereinbefore provided, and shall check thereon the names of all persons whose votes are received. At all elections the names of such officers as each voter is entitled and shall choose to vote for, shall be printed or written on one piece of paper. A ballot box of the usual construction shall be provided by the common council for each ward, and each person offering to vote shall deposit his vote on the lid of such box. The presiding officer shall receive and deposit in the box the ballots of all persons whose names are found on their voting lists by the two inspectors, and none others. At the expiration of the time allotted for voting, the presiding officer shall open the ballot box, publicly count the votes with the aid of the inspectors, or their deputies, and declare the result in open meeting. Immediately thereafter a certificate of the result, signed by the presiding officer and the two inspectors shall be transmitted, together with the voting lists, and the ballot box containing the ballots received, to the city clerk, which certificate shall be evidence of the vote in such ward. The city clerk shall enter the returns from each ward upon the city records and publish the same in the succeeding issue of at least one newspaper of said city, and shall therein declare those persons receiving the largest number of votes for their respective offices to be elected thereto. The presiding officer shall have all the power for the preservation of peace and good order in such meetings, as are by law conferred upon the moderator of town meetings. Any person whose name is not on such list as an elector of said city in such ward who shall vote for any officer of said city, or any person who shall vote or attempt to vote on or in the name of any other person whose name is on said list, shall be punished by a fine of not less than fifty dollars, nor more than one hundred dollars, or by imprisonment in the county jail not exceeding three months, or by such fine and imprisonment both. If either of said registrars shall, without just or reason-

2

able cause, refuse or neglect to discharge any of the duties herein prescribed, he shall, on conviction, be punished by a fine of three hundred dollars; and if any person other than the registrars shall make any alteration by addition, erasure, or otherwise, in the list prepared by the registrars, or if the presiding officer in any of said wards at any annual or special election, or any other person having charge of the ballot box in any of the wards aforesaid, at any such annual or special election, shall allow any person to deposit his vote therein whose name is not on the registry list of said ward, he shall be punished by a fine of not less than fifty dollars nor more than one hundred dollars, or by imprisonment in the county jail not less than three months, or by such fine and imprisonment both.

SEC. 9.   Every officer of the city shall be sworn before entering upon the duties of his office.   The form of the oath to be taken by the clerk shall be as follows: " You, A. B., do solemnly swear that you will faithfully perform the duties of the office of clerk of the city of New Britain so long as you are the clerk thereof, that you will make true entries and records of all the votes and proceedings of said city and of the common council thereof, and of such other matters as by law or the ordinances of said city are to be recorded in your office, and that you will deliver true copies of the records in your office when they shall be required of you, on the receipt of lawful fees therefor, so help you God," which oath shall be administered to such clerk by a justice of the peace for the county of Hartford, and thereafter said city clerk shall administer to all the other officers of said city the following oath:—" You solemnly swear that you will faithfully and honestly perform the office of   for the city of New Britain, to the best of your judgment and skill, so help you God," and shall forthwith enter the fact of such administration upon the city records.

SEC. 10.   The mayor of said city shall be the chief executive magistrate thereof, and it shall be his duty to be vigilant in causing the laws thereof to be enforced.   He shall preside at all meetings of the common council and all business meetings of the city. He shall have power to administer oaths, to take depositions and the acknowledgment of deeds.   He shall be conservator of the peace of said city, and shall have authority, with force and strong hand when necessary, to suppress all tumults, riots and unlawful assemblies, and to arrest, without warrant, and commit to the city prison for a time not exceeding twenty-four hours, any person or persons who may [be] detected in quarreling, brawling or otherwise behaving in a disorderly manner, to the disturbance of the public peace in said city. He shall also have power to enter into any house, building, or place, in which he may suspect any disorderly or vagrant persons to be assembled, and if any such are found therein, to command them to immediately disperse, and in case of neglect or refusal to obey such command, to commit any such person to the city prison for a term not exceeding twenty-four hours; and he shall be authorized to exercise within the limits of said city all the powers given to sheriffs, and other officers, by the one hundred and eleventh and one hundred and twelfth sections of an act entitled "An Act concerning crimes and punishments," and he may at all times require the aid of any sheriff, deputy sheriff, constable, watchman or policeman, or any or all of them together, with such other aid as may be necessary; and whenever he shall have reason to believe that great opposition will be made to the execution of his authority, he shall have power to call out the active militia of said city, or any portion of the same, and may exert all the force necessary to enable him to execute the laws within said city. It shall also be the duty of the mayor to recommend the adoption of all such measures connected with the police, security, health, cleanliness, and ornament of the city, and the improvement of its government and finances as he shall deem expedient, to communicate to the common council, at any meeting of that body during the month of March,* in each year, a general statement of the situation, state and condition of the city in relation to its government, finances, and improvements; which report shall, within five days thereafter be entered in the records of the common council, and published in such manner as said common council shall order. It shall be the further duty of the mayor to discharge all duties imposed upon him by the charter and ordinances of the city, the laws of this state and of the United States.

Sec. 11. If any person shall hinder, obstruct, resist, or abuse the mayor in the execution of the duties of his office, and when commanded to assist therein, shall refuse or unreasonably neglect so to do, such offender shall pay a fine not exceeding one hundred dollars, or be imprisoned in the county jail not exceeding six

* Altered to April, by amendment of June 19, 1876.

months, or suffer such fine and imprisonment both, at the discretion of the court having cognizance of the offense.

SEC. 12. The pay of members of the active militia during service under the call of the mayor as aforesaid, and the penalty for refusing to perform such service, shall be the same as is provided in such cases in the act entitled "An Act relating to sheriffs."

SEC. 13. Whenever there shall be a vacancy in the office of mayor, or whenever the mayor shall be absent from the city, or prevented by sickness or other cause from attending to the duties of his office, the alderman highest in rank, present in said city, shall act as mayor, and shall possess, exercise, and enjoy all the rights, powers, and duties of the mayor during the continuance of such vacancy, absence, or inability.

SEC. 14. The clerk of said city shall also be clerk of said common council, and shall make and keep true records of all the votes and proceedings of said city and of said common council. He shall cause the ordinances of said city to be published according to law, and when they shall have been so published, shall enter upon the records of said common council his certificate of the fact of such publication, including the date thereof. He shall also make, upon the records of said common council, record of his own acts in serving notices of orders passed by said common council. Said clerk shall also do and perform all such duties as may be required of him by this act, or by any order, vote or ordinance of said common council. All records of said clerk shall have the same validity as the records of town clerks, and shall be, either by themselves or by a copy certified by said clerk, evidence in all courts of the truth of the matters therein recorded.

SEC. 15. The common council may at any time appoint an assistant clerk, who, after having taken the oath by law provided for the clerk of said city, shall, in the absence or disability of said clerk, have power to perform all the duties of his office; and all records and acts of said assistant shall have the same validity as the records and the acts of said city clerk.

SEC. 16. The treasurer of said city shall have the same relative powers and responsibilities in said city as town treasurers have in their respective towns; he shall annually, in the month of March,* report to the common council, at any meeting of that body during

---

* Altered to April, by amendment of June 19, 1876.

said month, a detailed statement of the receipts of money into the treasury, and the expenditures therefrom during the year ending with the last day of February * previous thereto, together with an accurate statement of the existing state of the treasury; which report, having been audited by a committee appointed by the common council, shall be recorded within five days, and be published in such manner as the common council shall direct, together with the auditing committee's certificate, under oath concerning the same. He shall pay all orders of the city auditor, and shall also comply with all ordinances and orders that may be made concerning his office by the common council.

SEC. 17. The auditor of said city shall draw his orders on the treasurer thereof for the payment only of such bills as shall have been ordered to be paid by the common council.

SEC. 18. The sheriff of said city shall, within the limits thereof, have the same power and authority as sheriffs of counties, and shall be liable to the same suits and penalties for neglect of duty, and the said city shall be liable for the default of such sheriff in his office. Said sheriff shall attend upon the city court, when sitting for the transaction of civil business only.

SEC. 19. The collector of said city shall collect every tax duly laid by said city, and having received a warrant for that purpose signed by the mayor or one of the aldermen of said city, shall have the same power as collectors of town taxes now have, and shall be accountable to said city, and in case said collector shall not perform his trust, then on complaint of the common council, the mayor shall issue his warrant under his hand directed to the sheriff of said city, to collect out of the estate of the negligent collector the sum due from him as previously ascertained by said common council.

SEC. 20. The treasurer, collector, clerk of the city court, and sheriff shall severally give bonds with surety to the mayor of the city and his successors in office, in such amount, manner and form as the ordinances of said city shall prescribe, for the faithful performance of the duties of their respective offices, and in case of the refusal or neglect of either of said officers to give such bond, his office shall be deemed vacant by such refusal or neglect, and on a declaration to that effect being made by the common council, said city may proceed to elect another in his stead in the manner hereinbefore provided.

---

* Altered to March, by amendment of June 19, 1876.

Sec. 21. The mayor, aldermen, and councilmen of the said city shall constitute and be a body known as the common council of the city of New Britain. All meetings of said common council duly warned and held, at which a majority of the members are present, shall be valid meetings, and may proceed to transact any business properly before them, and all meetings at which less than a majority of said council are present shall have power to adjourn to such time as they see fit. All acts of said common council at any meeting, shall be done by a major vote of all the members present.

Sec. 22. The common council shall have power, under the restrictions otherwise provided in this act, to make such orders or ordinances as they see fit in relation to the following subjects within the limits of said city, to wit: nuisances of all kinds in the said city, and their summary abatement by any person by them appointed therefor; sinks, cess-pools, gutters, drains, sewers, privies, barns, stables, hog-pens, slaughter-houses, deposits of filth and rubbish; the going at large in the streets of animals or fowls of every description; the storing or piling of lumber; the erection and use of steam boilers; the keeping, sale and use of gunpowder, fire-works, nitro-glycerine, or other similar explosive substances, and the conveyance thereof through any portion of the city; the preservation of the city from damage by fire;* the markets and commerce of the city; the inspection of produce brought into the city for sale or transportation; the sale or offering for sale of un-wholesome meat, vegetables, produce, or food of any kind; the streets, highways, alleys, walks, and public grounds, and the preservation of all trees and shrubbery therein; keeping the same free from snow, ice, rubbish, or obstruction of any kind; the laying out, altering, constructing, grading, and repair of such streets, alleys, highways, walks and public grounds; the naming of all public streets, and the numbering of all lots thereon; the public water works and the management of the same; trespasses in gardens, cemeteries, and other enclosures; the cleaning of chimneys; burying-grounds and burials; the protection of all buildings from defacement or injury; the marching and parading of military and fire companies, and processions of every kind in the public streets; public assemblages, receptions, celebrations, shows, and music; the speed of animals, vehicles, and railroad trains; the manner of

---

*Amended June 19, 1876.

warning meetings of said city, and of the common council, and the times and places of such meetings; the establishment and maintenance of a police force; the preservation of order, the observance and enforcement of the laws of the state and the ordinances of the city by means of such police force; the mode of taxation as to taxes levied by said city; the licensing and regulating of public hacks and carriages, and the charges of hackmen, public drivers, cartmen, and truckmen; the finances and property, real and personal, of the city; and the borrowing of money by the city for any purpose for which the city is authorized to lay taxes by this act; the authentication, execution and delivery of deeds, grants, and releases of the city property; the erection of lamp-posts, and the public lighting of the streets; the excavation or opening of streets, highways and public grounds, for public or private purposes, and the location of any work thereon, whether temporary or permanent, upon or under the surface thereof, the depositing therein of building materials of any description, and the removal of buildings upon or through the same; the form of proceedings in taking land for public use not otherwise prescribed in this act; the preservation of public peace and order, the prevention and quelling of tumultuous noises, riots and disorderly assemblages; the conferring upon the mayor and police officers of the city or town constables of all the powers necessary for such purposes; the prohibition, restraining, licensing, and regulation of public sports, exhibitions, and performances; the punishment of the resistance, hindrance, or obstruction of public officers in the discharge of their duties; the filling of vacancies in any office appertaining to the city not otherwise provided for in this act; the election or appointment of city surveyors, coroners, street commissioners, water commissioners, public weighers, officers of the fire department, sealers of weights and measures, health officers, inspectors of articles offered for sale, and such other functionaries as are proper for the administration of the affairs of the city; the mode of keeping the accounts of said city; the conducting of all elections in matters not expressly regulated by this act, and the prevention and punishment of illegal voting thereat; the salaries and fees of all officers of said city, provided that no mayor, alderman, or councilman shall receive any fee, salary, compensation, or reward, for services as such mayor, alderman, or councilman, until the said city shall have a popula tion of twenty-five thousand inhabitants; the particular duties of all officers not expressly defined by this act; the removal of any officer on account of conviction of malfeasance in office; bathing in places exposed to public view; restraining cruelty to animals; licensing and regulating peddling and auctions; the erection of awning posts and the projection of signs, banners, and flags over, on or in any highway or street; the seal of said city; and said common council may prescribe penalties and forfeitures of goods and chattels for the violation of any such orders and ordinances, which penalties and forfeitures may be recovered by the attorney of the city, in an action of debt or other proper action brought in the name of the city of New Britain, before the city court of said city, for the use of the city treasury. The violation of any ordinance or order relative to nuisances injurious to health, illegal voting, obstructions to highways, (if malicious,) illegal charges of hackmen, weights and measures, or any order or ordinance designated to prevent vice, immorality, or disorder, or the resistance of officers, shall be a misdemeanor, and may be prosecuted as such before the police court of said city, like other offenses, and said court may inflict thereon the penalty named in such ordinance or order, and grant a warrant for the execution of the same; *provided*, that no penalty or forfeiture of goods other than such as shall indirectly accrue from the abatement of nuisances, shall exceed the sum of fifty dollars for a single offense.

SEC. 23. Every vote, resolution, order, or ordinance passed by said common council, shall be submitted to the mayor or acting mayor for his approval, and if such vote, resolution, order, or ordinance shall be disapproved by him, the same shall be returned to the common council at their next meeting, (whether an adjourned, a regular, or a special meeting,) with his objections thereto in writing, and if a majority * of said common council shall again pass such vote, resolution, order, or ordinance, the same shall be valid, as if the same had been approved by the mayor.

SEC. 24. Within sixty days after any ordinance has been passed, the mayor may call, and if requested in writing by five members of the common council, and thirty other voters of the city, he shall call a special meeting of the voters of the city to approve or disapprove said ordinance, to be held at such time and place, within ten days thereafter, as the mayor in said call shall designate. Such call shall be by notice published in a newspaper

---

* Altered to two-thirds by amendment of June 17, 1874.

of the city, and shall recite the ordinance to be acted upon by
such meeting. If a majority of the voters of the city present and
voting at such meeting shall vote to disapprove said ordinance, it
shall from that time be repealed and void, otherwise it shall continue in force.

SEC. 25. No member of the common council shall, during
the period for which he was elected, be appointed to or hold any
office, the emoluments of which are to be paid from the city
treasury ; nor shall he become, while a member of the common
council, directly or indirectly, interested in any contract, the
expense or consideration of which is to be paid under any vote or
resolution of the common council ; nor shall he be appointed or
permitted to act in carrying into effect any vote, resolution, or
matter whatever, of a local description, as committee or otherwise, in which he has a direct or special pecuniary interest, or
where his property will be directly or especially affected thereby.

SEC. 26. Said common council may make orders granting
appropriations to defray the legitimate expenses of said city. The
vote upon any such order shall, upon the request of any member
of said common council present, be taken by yeas and nays. At
the meeting whereat any such order shall be made, the mayor,
or in his absence, the alderman highest in rank, present, may
suspend, and if requested so to do by two aldermen and five
councilmen, shall at all events suspend said order. Any order so
suspended shall have no validity until it shall be approved by a
meeting of the electors of said city : and whenever such order
shall have been so suspended, the mayor (or the said alderman
highest in rank, present, as the case may be) shall call a meeting
of said electors to be held within ten days from the passage of
such order to approve or disapprove the same. If said meeting shall approve of said order, the same shall thereupon take
effect and thereafter be in full force, otherwise void.*

SEC. 27. The common council shall have power to prescribe
limits in said city within which it shall not be lawful for any person to erect or station any building, or addition to a building,
unless the outer walls and roof are composed of incombustible
materials, and said council shall enforce the observance of such
power by appropriate ordinances.

SEC. 28. The common council of said city shall have power

---

* Amended June 17, 1874.

3

to designate a line or lines on the land adjoining any highway or street in said city, between which line and said highway or street no building or part thereof shall be erected or stationed ; *provided*, such line shall not be more than fifteen feet distant from said highway or street. And any person who shall erect or station any building or part of a building between any line so designated, and the highway or street, shall forfeit and pay for the use of said city a fine not exceeding one hundred dollars, and in addition all such buildings shall be assessed four-fold in the list of ratable estate in said city. Said fine may be recovered in an action of debt or other proper action brought in the name of the said city before the city court thereof.

Sec. 29. The common council shall have power to lay out, construct and repair sewers and drains wherever they may deem the same necessary through or along any street, highway, public or private grounds, and to assess such portions as they may deem reasonable of the cost of any such sewer or drain upon the property for the carrying off the sewerage, surface or other drainage of which such sewer or drain may be constructed, or which may be in any way improved or benefited thereby, and the sums so assessed shall be a lien upon the said property, and may be foreclosed or collected as provided in section thirty-seven of this act. No person shall construct any drain or sewer of any kind upon and from any premises in said city, to or upon any highway or street in said city, or use or permit any such sewer or drain to be used without the permission of the common council ; and any person so constructing such drain or sewer, or using or permitting such to be used without such permission, shall forfeit and pay to the use of said city a fine of ten dollars for such construction, and a like amount for each day that such drain or sewer is so used or permitted to be used.*

Sec. 30. The common council shall have power, from time to time, to designate and fix the course, width, height, and grade of all sidewalks and gutters upon the streets and highways of said city, and may, at the expense of said city, cause any of the crosswalks in said city to be raised, flagged, paved, or made in a suitable manner.

Sec. 31. Said common council may, from time to time, order the owner or owners of the land and buildings fronting on such sidewalks and gutters, at their own expense, to make such sidewalks and gutters on their several fronts, according to the course,

---

* Amended June 9, 1874, and June 24, 1875.

width, height and grade designated as aforesaid ; and also to curb, flag or pave the same in such manner as the common council shall direct ; and also to provide and erect such railings or guards upon and along said walks as public safety may require. And said common council may limit such time as they may deem reasonable for so fencing, paving, or flagging, railing, and curbing such sidewalks and gutters as aforesaid, among the different persons having an interest in the lands or buildings holden as aforesaid; and whenever the owner or owners of any land or buildings shall not reside within the limits of the city, notice in writing to the occupant or occupants or persons having the care thereof, of any such order shall be sufficient notice thereof to all persons interested therein.*

SEC. 32. If any owner or owners of any such land or buildings shall neglect to make, pave, rail, flag, or curb any such sidewalk or gutter, in such manner, and within such time as the common council shall direct and limit, the said common council may appoint and employ some suitable person to do the same, and may adjust and liquidate the expense thereof, and order the same to be paid by such owner or owners neglecting as aforesaid. In cases where the land or buildings fronting such sidewalks or gutters shall be holden for a term of years, or any other estate less than a fee simple, said common council may, by their order, apportion in such manner as they shall judge right, the expense of raising, grading, forming, flagging, paving or making such sidewalks, and gutters, among the different persons having an interest in the land or building holden as aforesaid. Thereupon the mayor of said city may issue a warrant of distress, authorizing the city collector to collect of said owner or owners the sums ordered to be paid by them respectively as aforesaid, and such sums, with the interest thereon, shall be a lien or real incumbrance upon the land and buildings in reference to which such sums shall have been expended, to be enforced in like manner as if said lands and buildings were mortgaged to said city to secure the payment thereof.

SEC. 33. The common council of said city shall have sole and exclusive authority and control over all streets and highways, and over all parts of streets and highways, now or hereafter existing within the limits of the said city, and shall have sole and

---

* Amended June 17, 1874.

exclusive power to lay out, open, make, discontinue, alter, repair, maintain, grade, and drain all highways and streets now existing, or hereafter to be made, or discontinued within the limits of said city ; and no person shall open within the limits of said city any public way, except under and by virtue of an order of said common council ; and said common council shall have power to elect, annually, a street commissioner for said city, who shall hold his office for one year from and after his election ; and said common council shall define by proper ordinances and orders the powers and duties of the commissioner, and shall fix and designate his compensation.

SEC. 34.   In all cases when a tax shall be laid and collected, or a sum of money shall be appropriated by the town of New Britain for the purpose of making and repairing the highways and roads in said town, it shall be the duty of the selectmen of said town, together with an equal number of the senior aldermen of said city, to determine by a major vote of the whole number, the portion thereof which shall be applied for the making and support of the highways of said town, within the limits of said city ; and in case the selectmen and aldermen cannot agree by a major vote, as aforesaid, upon such apportionment, the county commissioner of Hartford County. residing nearest to said city, shall be called in to give a deciding vote.   The sum thus apportioned shall be paid into the treasury of said city ; and said town shall not be obliged to make or repair any highway in the limits of said city ; *provided always*, that the town of New Britain shall be liable to make and repair all bridges in said town to the same extent as if this act had not been passed.

SEC. 35.   Before the common council shall determine to lay out, alter, extend, enlarge, discontinue, or exchange any highway, street, public walk, or public avenue, or designate any building line in said city, they shall cause a notice, signed by the mayor of said city, or the clerk of said council, describing in general terms such proposed layout or alteration, or designation, and specifying a time and place when and where, all persons whose land is proposed to be taken therefor, may appear and be heard by said common council in relation thereto—to be published not less than two times in a newspaper published in said city, at least ten days before the time fixed in said notice for such hearing ; and such publication of said notice shall be legal and sufficient notice to all persons and corporations whose land is proposed to be taken by such layout or alteration. At the time and place mentioned in said notice, and at any meeting adjourned therefrom, said common council shall hear all the parties in interest, who may appear and desire to be heard in relation thereto.

SEC. 36. If after such hearing said common council shall resolve to lay out, alter, extend, enlarge, discontinue, or exchange such street, highway, walk, or avenue, or designate such building line or lines, they shall appoint a committee, whose duty it shall be to make such layout or alteration, and designate such building line or lines, and report in writing their doings to said common council, which report shall embody a descriptive survey of such street, highway, walk, avenue, or line or lines designated. If said report shall be accepted and approved by said common council, and said common council and the parties in interest cannot agree as to the damages and benefits to be assessed, the mayor, or, in his absence or inability to act. the alderman highest in rank present in said city, shall appoint three judicious and disinterested freeholders of said city to estimate and appraise the damages, or benefits, as the case may be, resulting or accruing to any person, or persons, from the taking of such land for public use as aforesaid, or from such layout, alteration, extension, enlargement, discontinuance, exchange, or designation of such line or lines ; said freeholders shall be sworn to a faithful and impartial discharge of the duties of said appointment, and a certificate of such appointment, and the administration of such oath, shall be made, under the hand of the officer appointing them, and recorded in the records of the common council. Before making any such assessment of damages and benefits, said freeholders shall give reasonable notice to all persons interested of the time and place when and where they will meet for that purpose; such notice shall be deemed reasonable and sufficient if signed by the said freeholders, or a majority of them, and published in the same manner as provided to be done by the common council in section thirty-five of this act ; or if given in such other manner as the common council by ordinance may prescribe; said freeholders shall meet at the time and place designated in their said notice, and at such other times and places as they may adjourn therefrom, and shall hear all the parties in interest who may appear before them, and shall thereupon ascertain and determine what person or persons will be damaged by such taking of said land, or by such layout, alteration or designation of building

line or lines, and the amount thereof over and above any special
benefits such person or persons may receive therefrom; also what
other person or persons owning or interested in lands contiguous
to or in the vicinity of the proposed improvement will be specially
benefited by such taking of said land .or by such layout, alteration,
or designation of building line or lines, and the amount thereof
over and above any damages such person or persons may receive
therefrom; also what other person or persons owning or interested
as above will receive an equal amount of damages and benefits
thereby, and such freeholders shall report the amount of damages
and benefits thus ascertained and determined, and the names of
the persons to whom the same respectively appertain and belong,
with a general description of the property in respect to which
said benefits are assessed to the common council, who may accept
said report, or return the same to said freeholders for reconsideration and correction ; and upon the acceptance of said report, the
clerk of the common council shall record the same in the records
of the common council, *provided*, that the whole amount of benefits assessed for any particular layout, alteration, or designation,
shall not exceed the whole amount of damages assessed on account
of the same layout, or alteration, or designation, and the estimated
cost of completing said improvement, which estimate said committee shall make and embody in their report ; said common
council shall cause a notice, signed by the mayor or clerk of said
common council, containing the names of the persons thus assessed,
with the amounts of their respective assessments, to be published
not less than two times in a newspaper published in said city, and
such publication shall be deemed to be legal and sufficient notice
to all persons interested in such assessments, and the same shall
thereupon immediately become due and payable. The common
council shall order the damages thus assessed and determined to
be paid to the persons to whom they respectively belong out of the
treasury of the city; *provided*, that if any person shall refuse or
neglect to receive the amount so found due and ordered to be paid
to him, the same shall be deposited in the city treasury, to be paid
to the person entitled to receive it whenever he shall apply for
the same. And the descriptive survey before mentioned, being
signed by the mayor, or senior alderman, and entered upon the
records of said common council, and the damages assessed having
been paid or deposited as aforesaid, said highway, street, public

walk, or building line, shall be and remain for the purpose for which it was laid out or designated.*

SEC. 37. The assessments of benefits so made shall be and remain a lien on real incumbrance upon the land upon which they are respectively made, and shall take precedence of all other liens or incumbrances thereon, (except taxes due the state,) and the lands, with the buildings thereon, on which any such lien may exist, shall be liable to be foreclosed in the same manner as if said lien were a mortgage on such lands and buildings in favor of said city, to secure the amount of such assessment ; *provided however*, that such lien shall not continue to exist for a period longer than sixty days after the last publication of the notice thereof as aforesaid ; unless, within that period, a certificate, signed by the mayor of said city or the clerk of said common council, describing the premises on which such lien exists and the amount claimed by said city as a lien thereon shall be lodged with the town clerk of the town of New Britain ; *and provided further*, that such lien shall cease to exist whenever a certificate to that effect, signed by the mayor or clerk of the common council for the time being, shall be lodged with said town clerk. All such certificates said town clerk shall record with deeds of land. And such assessments may also be collected by warrant, under the hand of the mayor of said city, in the same manner as town taxes are by law collected.

SEC. 38. All persons aggrieved by the estimate of freeholders of any damage caused by the layout, discontinuance, alteration or enlargement of any highway or street, or the designation of building lines, and all persons aggrieved by the assessment of benefits consequent thereon, or consequent upon the construction of any sewer or drain by the common council, may within ten days after notice of such estimate or assessment apply, by petition to any judge of the superior court,† for a re-estimate of such damages or a re-assessment of such sum ordered to be paid by them, giving reasonable notice in writing to the clerk of said city of the time and place of such application, and of the name of said judge, and said judge shall appoint three judicious and disinterested freeholders of the county of Hartford, who shall re-estimate said damages, or re-assess said sums ordered to be paid to or by the persons making such application, and make report of

* Amended July 1, 1873.
† Altered to Judge of the Court of Common Pleas, by Amendment of July 1, 1873.

their doings to said judge, who shall have authority for any cause he may deem sufficient to set aside said report, and order another estimate or assessment to be made, or make such other order therein as to justice shall appertain. If upon such application for re-estimate or re-assessment, the damages shall be increased, or the assessment of benefits shall be decreased, and the same be approved by said judge, the costs of application shall be paid by the said city, otherwise by the applicant.

SEC. 39. The common council of said city shall constitute a board of health in said city, and shall have, and may exercise all power and authority which they shall judge necessary and proper for the prevention of disease of any kind, and for the promotion of the health of the inhabitants of said city; may make and cause to be executed all orders for such purpose as they may deem proper, and may appoint health committees to carry the same into effect. And said common council, or the mayor of the city, or any member of such health committee, may cause all filthy and putrid substances of any kind which they shall think injurious to the health and cleanliness of the city to be removed at the expense of the proprietor or proprietors of the land or building upon or in which said substance may be, and for that purpose may enter upon or into all lands or buildings in said city ; and the mayor may issue a warrant of distress to the collector of the city to collect such expense of such person or persons.

SEC. 40. The court hitherto holden and existing under the name of the borough court of New Britain, shall continue to be holden under the name of the city court of New Britain, on the first Monday of every month, commencing at two o'clock in the afternoon of said day ; said court shall have power to adjourn from time to time, and shall have original and final jurisdiction of all civil cases, except as hereinafter provided; *provided*, either party live within the limits of the town of New Britain, and the matter in demand shall exceed the jurisdiction of a justice of the peace, and shall not exceed five hundred dollars; but said court shall have jurisdiction of all cases brought to recover penalties under the ordinances and orders of said city, or the provisions of this act. Said court shall have jurisdiction of all suits in equity brought before it, except for relief against any judgment rendered, or against any cause pending in the superior court, or in the court of common pleas in the county of Hartford, and may enquire into the facts by itself, or by a committee, and may proceed to final judgment and decree, and enforce the same according to the rules of equity; *provided* the cause of the proceedings in equity originated, and one or both of the parties reside within the limits of said town of New Britain, and the premises in question, in cases of foreclosure or other proceedings relating to real estate, shall be situated in said town; and said court shall have the same power and authority and shall proceed in the same manner as superior courts now or hereafter shall have power to proceed. The course of practice and manner of proceeding in said court shall be conformable to that in the superior court so far as is practicable, and all statutory provisions regarding the trial, disposition of, and mode of proceeding in cases in the superior court shall be applicable, so far as is practicable to cases in said city court except otherwise herein provided.*

Sec. 41. Whenever an appeal shall be taken from the judgment rendered in any case by a justice of the peace for the county of Hartford residing in the town of New Britain in said county, the same shall be taken to the next term of the city court † to be held within and for the city of New Britain ; *provided*, either party reside within the limits of said town of New Britain, and said justice of the peace, from whose judgment an appeal is so taken, shall certify both upon the original writ and the copy in the appeal that one or both of the parties live within the limits of said town ; and bonds for prosecution shall be taken to the adverse party in the same manner as is now by law provided in appeals to the superior court ; and said·appeal shall be entered upon the docket of said city court, and said city court may proceed to trial and final judgment, and grant and enforce execution in the same manner as is now by law provided in like appeals in the court of common pleas for said Hartford county.

Sec. 42. Whenever final judgment or decree is rendered in said city court in any cause where said city court has final jurisdiction, either party, in the same term and within five days after final judgment, may make and present to said court a motion for a new trial, stating therein the questions of law, or a motion in error for questions arising on the record of such proceedings ; and if said court shall be of opinion that such motion is not intended for delay, and that the questions are such as to entitle the party to a revision thereof, said court shall reserve such

---

* Amended July 19, 1876.
† Altered to Court of Common Pleas; General Statutes, Revision of 1875, p. 415.

4

motion for a new trial for the opinion of the superior court next to be holden at Hartford, and shall allow such motion in error and transmit such record to said superior court in the same manner and according to the same rules and'regulations as are by law provided in the case of similar motions made in the superior court ; and said superior court shall at its first term thereafter proceed to hear and determine the issues presented under such motion for a new trial or in error, in the same manner and according to the same rules and regulations as is now by law provided for the supreme court of errors in like cases.

SEC. 43.   There shall be a judge for said court, who shall be chosen by the general assembly ;* he shall enter upon the duties of his office on the first Monday of July next following his said election, and shall hold the same for the period of one † year, and until another is chosen and sworn in his stead, and the oath to be taken by said judge shall be the same, *mutatis mutandis*, as the oath provided by law to be taken by executive and judicial officers ; *provided*, that in case of the death or resignation of said judge, the governor shall appoint some person to fill the vacancy occasioned thereby, until the first Monday of July next thereafter.

SEC. 44.   Said court shall have power to appoint and swear a clerk of said court, to continue in office during the pleasure of said court, who shall as to matters relative to his office as clerk of said court, have the same power and authority, and be entitled to the same fees as clerks of superior courts, and the oath to be taken by the clerk shall be the same, *mutatis mutandis*, as the oath provided by law to be taken by clerks of superior courts. It shall be the duty of the clerk of said city court, upon the allowance of any appeal from said court, to make a true and attested copy of the record in such cause for the party appealing, and he shall receive therefor such fees as are or may be allowed by law to the clerks of superior courts for copies.

SEC. 45.   The common council of said city of New Britain shall have the power to appoint an attorney for said city, also an assistant attorney to act in his absence, or at his request, both of whom shall be sworn to a faithful discharge of the duties of their office; and such attorney shall have power to sue and prosecute for all penalties for the breach of any of the by-laws of said city in the name of the city, by proper action before said city court,

---

* Amended July 30, 1872.
† Altered to two by Constitutional Amendment, 1876.

and shall appear in all cases brought for or against said city of New Britain.

SEC. 46. The process in all actions brought to said city court shall be the same as process to the superior courts ; ' which process may be signed by any officer of this state authorized to sign writs and judicial processes, or by the judge or clerk of said city court, and may be served by any officer duly qualified under the laws of this state to serve writs and other judicial processes, or the sheriff of said city, or by an indifferent person deputed to serve the same, to whom directed according to law and the provisions of this act; and all bonds of prosecution taken by any of the officers empowered to sign writs shall be good and effectual, and bonds of prosecution, special bail, and bonds for writs of error, shall be taken to the adverse party.

SEC. 47. All writs shall be served at least twelve days before the sitting of the court to which the same may be returnable ; and all writs returnable to said court shall be returned to the clerk thereof on or before the Friday preceding the term of court to which the same may be returnable.

SEC. 48. The common council of said city shall provide a suitable room, and such other accommodations for said city court, including records, blanks, stationery, and so forth, contemplated by this act, as said judge may deem necessary.

'SEC. 49. The salary * of said judge and the time and manner of paying the same shall be fixed by the common council of said city, and shall be in lieu of all fees whatsoever for services as such judge; and shall be paid from the city treasury in such manner as shall be provided by the ordinances of said city for paying money from said treasury. All fees arising from said court (except clerks' fees) shall be paid over by the clerk of said court to the city treasurer; said clerk may draw his order upon the city treasurer for all jury, witness' and officers' fees, or pay the same from any funds he may have in his hands; he shall render his account of the same under oath to the treasurer of said city as often as once each year.

SEC. 50. Whenever either party to any cause pending before said city court desire the same to be determined by jury, said party shall so notify the clerk of said court in writing within the first three days of the term to which said cause is brought, and

---

* Amended July 2, 1875.

the said cause in such case shall be entered on the jury docket of said court for trial. Whenever, in the opinion of the judge, a jury shall be needed to attend upon said court, then by his direction the clerk shall issue a warrant directed to the sheriff of said city or either of the constables of said town, commanding the officer receiving such warrant to draw and summon such jury, and such officer shall thereupon proceed in the manner hereinafter provided.

SEC. 51. The police court hitherto established within and for the borough of New Britain, shall be and remain a police court within and for said city of New Britain. The judge of the city court for said city shall be judge of said police court, which said judge shall have and exercise, in addition to the jurisdiction and powers relating to criminal cases, now vested in the justices of the peace residing in the town of New Britain, the other powers and duties conferred and imposed on such police judge by this act. In case said judge shall at any time be unable or disqualified to act in any cause, or in case the duties of the office shall be too great for him reasonably to perform, he may designate and request in writing, any justice of the peace, resident within said city, to act as his substitute, and said justice, while so acting under such request; shall have the same powers as such judge would have in like case ; and such written request shall be recorded and kept with the records of said court by the clerk of the same.

SEC. 52. From and after the time when said judge shall commence the discharge of his official duties, no person or persons (other than said judge) within the limits of said city and town, except when acting as substitute, as hereinbefore provided, or may be provided in the subsequent sections of this act, shall have, use, or exercise any of the powers specified and mentioned in the preceding section of this act, except in cases herein specially provided for ; *provided*, that nothing in this act shall be so construed as to prohibit any magistrate now authorized by law to issue warrants for the arrest of offenders, from issuing the same hereafter, or to prohibit justices of the peace from discharging any ministerial duty or office now by law imposed upon them, but all warrants issued on account of any offense committed within the jurisdiction of said police court shall command the officer serving the same to arrest the offender and bring him before the said police court, who shall deal with him in the same manner, whether such warrant shall have been issued by any magistrate as aforesaid, or by and from said police court.

SEC. 53. No such judge shall be disqualified to sit in any *qui tam* or other penal action or prosecution from which a penalty may accrue to the treasurer of said city, by reason of his being a resident in said city and liable to taxation therein.

SEC. 54. Said police court shall have authority, subject to the provisions of this act, to hear and determine charges for crimes and misdemeanors committed within the limits of the town and city of New Britain, the punishment of which, as prescribed by law, does not exceed a fine of two hundred dollars, or six months imprisonment in a common jail, county, or town workhouse, or such fine and imprisonment both. And in all such cases said court may proceed to trial, render judgment thereon, and grant a warrant for the execution thereof, according to law; but in all cases the person convicted may appeal from the judgment of said police court to the superior court next to be holden in the county of Hartford, except when the conviction shall be for the crime of drunkenness, profane swearing, and sabbath breaking; *provided* he gives bonds with good and sufficient surety, on the appeal, as said police court shall order, payable to the treasurer of the state of Connecticut, or the treasurer of the county of Hartford, as the law in each case may require, conditioned for the appearance of the person so convicted before said superior court to answer concerning the offense whereof he stands charged, and to abide the judgment that may be rendered by the said superior court. If the crime charged against the accused shall in any case be of so aggravated a nature as to require a greater punishment than is above specified, the accused shall be by said police court bound over to the next superior court having cognizance of the offense, in the manner provided by law in cases of binding over by justices of the peace, and in all cases not bailable, said court shall proceed in the same manner as now provided by law in like cases.

SEC. 55. The clerk of the city court for said city shall be the clerk of said police court; said clerk shall keep a record of its proceedings, which shall be open during business hours for public inspection, and shall receive all fines, penalties, and costs, and moneys founded on or received by reason of all and any convictions or judgments had and rendered by said police court and belonging to said city, and shall account for the same to and with the treasurer of said city in writing, under oath, on the first Monday of July, or within ten days thereafter, in each year, and as often as the common council of said city shall order, and shall pay the same into the treasury within thirty days of the time of accounting with the treasurer as aforesaid ; said treasurer shall lodge said account on file, and keep the same for the use of said city. The salaries of said judge and of said clerk, and the time and manner of paying the same shall be fixed by the common council of said city, and such salary shall be in lieu of all fees whatsoever for criminal business. And said clerk shall, before entering upon the duties of his office, execute a bond as hereinbefore prescribed, conditioned that he shall faithfully render an account in writing, under oath, to the treasurer of said city, and pay over all fines, penalties, fees and costs, belonging to said city, that shall come into the hands of said clerk, into the treasury of said city, as is hereinbefore provided.

Sec. 56.. The common council of said city shall provide a court room and such other accommodation for said police court as said judge shall deem necessary, including record books, blanks, stationery. and so forth ; and said court shall be open for the transaction of business every day except Sundays, at *nine o'clock in the forenoon, and for so long a time as shall be necessary to transact all necessary business before said court during said day.

Sec. 57. Presentments or complaints in any criminal matter cognizable by said police court, may be made to the same by any grand juror of the town of New Britain, or the attorney or assistant attorney for the city of New Britain ; and said police court, and the clerk thereof, shall exercise the same powers in relation to the issuing of process against persons so complained of, and the granting of summons or capias for witnesses, as are conferred by law upon justices of peace in such cases.

Sec. 58. Before entering upon the trial of any criminal cause, the said police court may adjourn the hearing or trial thereof from time to time, not exceeding fifteen days, unless said court, upon good cause shown, may deem a longer time necessary, for the purpose of procuring material testimony, which time shall not exceed ninety days ; and said court, if the offense charged be bailable, shall take good and sufficient bail, if offered, for the appearance of the person charged, at the day to which the trial

---

* Altered to eight by Amendment of June 24, 1875.

or hearing is adjourned. If the case is within the final jurisdiction of said police court, the bond or recognizance shall be payable to the city treasurer, otherwise to the county or state treasurer, as the nature of the offense shall require.

Sec. 59. Said police court is hereby required to charge and tax for the use of the city of New Britain, in any criminal proceeding, such clerk fees as are now allowed by law to the clerks of the superior court, and two dollars for the trial of each case, and one dollar on each appeal, and the fees of the prosecuting officer, who shall make any complaint or presentment, shall be the same as those now provided by law for grand jurors of towns, and payable from the city treasury. And all such fees of the prosecuting officer, who shall make complaint, shall be taxed and received by the clerk in favor of the city of New Britain; said clerk may pay unto persons entitled to costs in any criminal prosecution, such costs as have of right accrued to them, taking their receipt therefor, but shall not pay costs to any person who shall not demand the same within six months after the same are taxed ; *provided*, that no part of said costs shall be received by or paid to any salaried officer of said city, for any service whatever, as witness or otherwise ; and said clerk may draw orders on the city treasurer for such sums as are necessary for the purpose hereinbefore indicated, or may pay the same out of the funds of the city in his hands.

Sec. 60. The said clerk shall receive all fines and costs imposed by said police court, and paid before commitment, and account for the same to the city treasurer, as hereinbefore provided; and all fines and costs paid after commitment shall be received by the keeper of the jail or of the workhouse where the offender shall be confined, and by such keeper paid to the treasurer of the city of New Britain, within thirty days after the same shall have been received by said keeper of said jail or workhouse.

Sec. 61. It shall be the duty of the city attorney to prosecute, in the name of the city treasurer, any of the bonds mentioned in this act, which are payable to such treasurer, within fifteen days after the same shall be forfeited, and account to and with the city treasurer for all sums received or recovered on such bonds except his taxable fees; and it is hereby made the duty of the clerk of said police court to give immediate information to the city attorney of the forfeiture of all bonds taken to the treasurer of said city, in pursuance of this act. And in case of the sickness of said police judge, or his absence from the city at any time when his services as such judge may be required, the clerk of said police court, or the city attorney, may, if they think proper, designate and request, in writing, any justice of the peace, resident within said city, to act in the place of said police judge, and said justice while so acting or when acting by previous request of the judge himself, shall have the same fees as are by law allowed to justices of the peace in criminal cases, which fees shall be paid in the same manner as costs are hereinbefore provided to be paid to persons entitled to receive them ; such written request shall be recorded by the clerk of said court, and kept with the records thereof; and such justice, while acting under such request shall have the same powers as the judge would have in the same case.

SEC. 62. The common council of the said city of New Britain may enter into any arrangement with the county commissioners of Hartford county, or with the inspectors of any workhouse within said county, to receive and keep all persons who may be sentenced to confinement in the common jail of said county, or in such workhouse by said police court; and it shall be the duty of the sheriff of Hartford county, his deputy, the sheriff of said city of New Britain, and of any constable of the town of New Britain, or either of the special constables, or policemen of said city of New Britain, to convey all persons so sentenced, without delay, to the appointed place of confinement, and deliver them to the keeper thereof, who shall receive and imprison such persons and employ them according to the rules, regulations, and discipline of such place of confinement, during the term for which they shall be severally sentenced and committed, or until they are discharged by law; but the said common council shall not have power to enter into any such agreement at any one time, for a longer period than two years.

SEC. 63. It shall be lawful for said police court, at its discretion, and in the manner provided by the public laws of this state, to order any person brought before said court on any criminal presentment, to be committed to any reform school, or other institution now or hereafter established within this state for juvenile offenders, and the proper officer of such institution shall receive and keep such person according to the rules and discipline of the same.

SEC. 64. Process issued by or returnable to said police court may be served by the sheriff of Hartford county, or his deputies, or any constable of the town of New Britain, or the sheriff, policeman, or any special constable of the city of New Britain, or any indifferent person deputed to serve the same, who shall severally receive the fees therefor, now prescribed by law for constables of towns for like service, and no more ; *provided*, no fee shall be paid to any salaried officer of said city for such service, but the legal fees therefor shall be taxed and paid to the clerk, for the city treasury, upon conviction of any person arrested ; *and provided further*, that the authority of the sheriff, or any special constable or policeman of said city, shall not extend beyond the limits of the town of New Britain, except as hereinbefore provided.*

SEC. 65. It shall be lawful for all officers hereby authorized to serve process issued by and returnable to the police court, and it shall be their duty to arrest without previous complaint and warrant, all such persons as are guilty of drunkenness, vagrancy, disorderly conduct, breaches of the peace, and common assault, when such offenses shall be committed within the limits of said town of New Britain, and such offenders shall be taken and apprehended in the act, or on the present information of others ; and it shall be lawful for said court to proceed to trial and render judgment, without previous complaint and warrant, upon persons so arrested, in the same manner as if they had been arrested upon process issued by said court.

SEC. 66. Whenever any person shall be arraigned before said police court for drunkenness, vagrancy, disorderly conduct or a breach of the peace, said court may indefinitely suspend judgment concerning him, whenever such forbearance shall seem to the court required, either by reason of the age of the accused, or the circumstances under which the offense was committed.

SEC. 67. Said police court may reduce or disallow fees taxable by said court, in cases where the negligence of any ministerial or informing officer, or the discharge of the accused for want of evidence, or the insufficiency of the service rendered, or other circumstances, shall render such reduction or disallowance expedient in the view of said court, in the exercise of its sound discretion.

SEC. 68. Sureties of the peace and for good behavior may be

---

* Amended July 20, 1875.

required by said police court, in such cases and in such manner
as justices of the peace are now authorized by law to require the
same ; *provided* the cause or occasion of requiring the same shall
arise within the limits of the town of New Britain.

SEC. 69. All fines, penalties and forfeitures incurred by a
violation of any of the provisions of this act, or any order or
ordinance of the common council of said city, shall be for the use
of said city, and may be recovered by an action of debt, or other
proper action in the name of the city, brought to said city court,
or by information of the city attorney made to said police court,
in the cases specified in the twenty-first [twenty-second] section of
this act, to be proceeded with in all respects as other actions
brought to said city court, or other informations brought to said
police court; *provided*, that no person shall be prosecuted both
civilly and criminally for the same act of breaking any order or
ordinance.

SEC. 70. The common council of said city of New Britain, on
the third Monday * in June, annually, shall meet and then choose
sixty or more electors of said city to serve as jurors at said city
court, and shall return the names of said jurors under the hand
of the mayor, if present, or in his absence, under the hand of
the senior alderman present at such meeting, to the clerk of said
city court, who shall write each juror's name thus chosen fairly
on a separate piece of paper, and roll up and put the same into
a box which he shall provide and keep for that purpose ; and
whenever the sheriff or either of the constables within the city of
said New Britain shall receive a warrant from the clerk of said
city court to summon a jury to appear before said court, the officer
receiving such warrant, taking with him one of the aldermen of
the city, shall repair to the said clerk's office, and there, in the
presence of such alderman and clerk, shall take out of said box
so many of said papers as his warrant shall direct; and the persons whose names shall be found written thereon shall be summoned to appear before the court to which the warrant is returnable, to serve as jurors; and in case of neglecting to attend shall
be liable to such penalties as shall by the ordinances of said city
be inflicted for such neglect. Authority to enact such ordinances
is hereby conferred upon the common council of said city of New
Britain; and in case any juror shall be challenged or excused, and

---

* Altered to Wednesday, by Amendment of July 1, 1873.

a panel can not be completed from the jurors summoned, the sheriff or other officer attending said court shall supply such deficiency by drawing, in the presence of the court, others out of said box, and summoning them to attend and serve until the panel shall be complete. The name of each juror that attends and serves in said court shall be again written on a separate piece of paper, and rolled up and put in another box, provided by the clerk for that purpose, and shall be liable to be drawn again only when there shall not, by reason of death, removal, or other causes, be a sufficient number in the first box to complete the panels for the year in which they are chosen to serve.

Sec. 71. Forms substantially like the following may be used in reference to the matters indicated in their titles, and shall be sufficient; but nothing in this section shall be construed as prohibiting the use of other forms in reference to the same matters, or as invalidating any other forms :

I. *Form of Ordinance.*

Be it ordained by the common council of the city of New Britain. Sec. 1, &c.

II. *Form of order under Section* 30.

Ordered, That (a or the) sidewalk (or gutter) on the side of　　　street, from　　　to　　　be　　　by the (proprietor or proprietors) of the lands fronting on said street, on that side thereof and between said points, to the acceptance of the street commissioner, before the　　　day of　　　A. D. 18

III. *Form of certificate of lien under Section* 37.

This certificate witnesseth, that the city of New Britain has a lien on certain land in said city, (and the buildings thereon,) owned in whole or in part by A. B., bounded and described as follows, to wit : (describe the premises) and that the amount claimed as a lien as aforesaid on said premises is dollars and　　　cents.

In witness whereof I have hereunto set my hand at said city, this　　　day of　　　A. D. 18　.

C. D., mayor (or city clerk) of city.

IV. Form of certificate of discharge of lien under Section 37.

This certificate witnesseth, that the lien heretofore claimed by the city of New Britain upon the premises owned in whole or in part by A. B., bounded and described as follows, to wit : (describe the premises) has ceased to exist.

In witness whereof, I have hereunto set my hand, at said city, this   day of   A. D. 18 .

C. D., mayor (or city clerk) of city.

V.   Form of an order of apportionment under Section 32.

Whereas, by an order of this common council, it has been made the duty of the proprietors of a certain piece of land, to wit : (describe it) to   (sidewalk or gutter) in front of said land ; and whereas, the said land is held by different persons, to wit : A. B., C. D., and E. F., in such a manner as to authorize this common council to apportion among said persons, pursuant to section thirty-one of the city charter, the expenses of executing said order ; and whereas, said expense is estimated at (or ascertained to be)   dollars and   cents. *Ordered,* that the said A. B. pay (state the fractional part) of said expense, and said C. D., (fractional part) of said expense, (and so on.)

VI.   Form of complaint for violation of order or ordinance.

To the honorable city police court for the city of New Britain, comes A. B., city attorney of said city, and on his oath of office, complaint and information makes, that since the incorporation of said city, to wit, on the   day of   A. D. 18 , and within the limits of said city,   of the town of in the county of   with force and arms (set forth the act complained of) against the peace, contrary to the ordinance (or order, as the case may be,) of said city in such case provided, and contrary to the statute in such case provided; therefore, the said city attorney prays process, and that the said   may be arrested, held to answer to this complaint, and be therein dealt with according to law.

Dated at said New Britain, this   day of   A. D. 18 .

A. B., city attorney.

VII.   Form of action to recover fine, penalty, &c.

To the sheriff of the city of New Britain : By authority of the state of Connecticut you are hereby commanded to summon A. B., of   , to appear before the city court of the city of New Britain, within said county, next to holden at the city court room in said city, on the first Monday of   , A. D. 18   , then and there to answer unto the city of New Britain, in a plea that to the plaintiff the defendant render the sum of   , which to the plaintiff the defendant owes, and from them unjustly detains, whereupon the plaintiff declares and says that, heretofore, to wit, on the   day of   , A. D. 18   , the said A. B. (state the act or negligence which subjects the defendant to the fine, penalty, or forfeiture to be collected.)   All of which was contrary to the ordinance of said city, entitled (give the title to the ordinance imposing the fine, penalty, or forfeiture.)   And the said defendant thereby became, and still is liable to forfeit and pay to the plaintiff, for the use of the city treasurer, the sum of   , recoverable in an action of debt on said ordinance.   Whereby an action hath accrued to the plaintiff, to demand and recover of the defendant, the sum of   , which to the plaintiff the defendant hath never paid, though often requested so to do.   All which is to the damage of the plaintiff in the sum of   , and therefore they bring their suit.   Hereof fail not, but due service and return make.   C. D., of said New Britain, is recognized in the sum of   dollars to prosecute, &c.   Dated at said New Britain this   day of   , A. D. 18   .

SEC. 72.   The common council shall annually, in the month of April, at their first meeting after the election on said second Monday of April, or at an adjourned meeting held the same month, elect by ballot, a captain of police, and not exceeding three active policemen; and such other supernumerary policemen as they shall deem proper, not exceeding twenty, shall also be appointed at said meeting, which officers shall hold their respective offices for the term of one year, and until others are chosen, and sworn in their stead.   In case either of said offices shall at any time become vacant by reason of death or otherwise, said common council may fill any such vacancy, and any person chosen to fill such vacancy shall hold said office until the next annual meeting following the day of his election, and until another be chosen to fill said office and sworn in his stead.*

---

* Amended July 1, 1873.

SEC. 73. The common council may make all needful rules and regulations for the government of the police force, may fix the amount of salaries, may call out the supernumerary police when they deem it necessary, and may authorize the mayor or captain of police to do the same, may fix the amount of their compensation while on duty, and to do any other lawful act to render the police force most efficient. Said police and supernumeraries, when on duty, shall have the same power within said city to pursue and secure offenders as constables have in their respective towns.

SEC. 74. The common council of said city shall have authority to control the fire companies at present organized in the borough of New Britain, together with all the lands, buildings, engines, and other apparatus now held by said borough and used for protection against fire. And they shall have power to form and control such other fire companies in said city as they may hereafter deem necessary, and to organize a fire department and appoint such officers for the same as they may deem expedient.

SEC. 75. All the powers relating to the water supply hitherto exercised by the warden and burgesses of the borough of New Britain under the act to supply the borough of New Britain with water for public and private purposes and the additions thereto and amendments thereof, are hereby vested in said common council, and all duties imposed and powers conferred upon the water commissioners of said borough are hereby imposed and conferred upon the water commissioners of said city; *provided, however,* that said commissioners shall be subjected to all orders and ordinances of the common council relating to introducing water into streets and districts before unsupplied, and to the use of such water for public purposes generally. Said common council shall annually in the month of May appoint three water commissioners who shall enter upon their duties on the first Monday in June in each year, and shall hold office for one year and until successors are appointed and qualified in their stead.*

The bonds commonly known as "water bonds," heretofore . issued by the borough of New Britain, under the various acts authorizing the same, together with all other obligations of said borough, and its inhabitants, are hereby expressly declared to be in full force and effect, and shall be obligatory upon said city and the inhabitants thereof, to the same extent that they have been heretofore obligatory upon said borough and its inhabitants.

---

* Amended May 26, 1875.

Sec. 76. Said city, in legal meeting assembled, shall have power to lay taxes on the polls and ratable estate within the limits of the city for such purposes as the city shall think proper, agreeable to the privileges in this act.

Sec. 77. This act shall come into effect on the second Monday of April, 1871, and all persons holding office under the charter of the borough of New Britain, at the end of the current official year of said borough, shall continue in their respective offices until the officers provided for in this act shall be elected and qualified. On said second Monday the first annual election of the city shall be held, and the registrars shall prepare for the same in the manner provided herein, and shall also appoint two inspectors of elections in each ward, who shall have all the powers conferred, and be subject to all the duties imposed upon inspectors of elections by this act, at said first election of said city ; and said first election shall be held in the several wards at such places as the inspectors shall designate by public notice in manner provided in section eight, and said inspectors shall provide ballot boxes for use at such elections.

Sec. 78. The first meeting of the common council of said city shall be called by the mayor, and all meetings of said council called by the mayor shall be valid and legal meetings, until said common council shall provide for the manner of calling meetings thereof ; *provided*, that the mayor shall cause actual notice to be given to each member of said common council of the time, and place of holding the meetings called by him as aforesaid.

Sec. 79. From and after the time when the provisions of this act go into effect, all other existing provisions of law enacted by any public act, for the special purpose of affecting the warden, burgesses and freemen of the borough of New Britain shall be inoperative, and are hereby declared to be, from and after such time, repealed : but said repeal shall not impair or affect any rights, privileges, or immunities vested in any person or body corporate, or any pecuniary obligations now attaching to said community; and all matters, civil or criminal, commenced by virtue of the provisions of law so repealed, and pending unfinished, when said repealing provisions take effect, may be prosecuted to final effect, in the same manner as if this act had not been passed; no offence committed, and no penalty or forfeiture incurred, and no tax or assessment laid or incurred, under any of the provisions of law herein repealed, or under any by-law made under any of said provisions, shall be in anywise affected by said repeal. The by-laws of said borough, in force on the second Monday of April, 1871, shall thereafter continue in force, notwithstanding any provisions of this act, until repealed by the common council of said city.

SEC. 80. This act shall be a public act.

SEC. 81. This act shall not take effect unless approved by the freemen of the borough of New Britain, at a special meeting duly warned and held within six months from the passage hereof, and George M. Landers, S. A. Moore, T. W. Stanley, James D. Frary, and S. C. Dunham, are hereby authorized and directed to call such meeting, by giving public notice thereof at least two weeks in the New Britain Record, and for a like time on the town post in said New Britain, and said call shall be valid if signed by any three of the abovenamed persons. At said meeting, those in favor of approving and adopting this act shall vote yes, and those opposing shall vote no. And if a majority of the freemen voting vote yes, this act shall thereupon become operative at the time hereinbefore fixed : but if the majority voting vote no, this act shall be of no force or effect.

Approved, July 15th, 1870.

AMENDMENTS.

AN ACT IN ADDITION TO AN ACT INCORPORATING THE CITY OF NEW BRITAIN.

Be it enacted by the Senate and House of Representatives in General Assembly convened:

SECTION 1. The common council of said city are hereby authorized, whenever in their opinion the public health or sewerage shall require such action, to take, occupy, and appropriate, in such manner as they shall, from time to time, deem expedient, any stream or part of a stream, natural or artificial, running in or through said city, and to straighten, deepen, or lower the same, or lower or remove any or all walls, dams, or other obstructions to the free and healthy flow of such stream or part of a stream, or enlarge or cause to be enlarged or lowered, any or all culverts, which at any season of the year cause the accumulation of stagnant water, or interrupt in any manner the free and healthy flow of any part of such stream.

SEC. 2. Whenever said common council shall take action under the foregoing power, they shall appoint a committee to prepare a descriptive survey of the improvement contemplated, with a careful estimate of the cost of completing the same, and to agree with the parties interested as to damages and special benefits on account of such improvement ; and the report of such survey and estimate having been accepted and recorded, and such agreement having been ratified, and the sums agreed upon as damages having been paid to the parties entitled thereto, or deposited to their credit in the city treasury, said city may go on to the completion of said improvement, and do all acts necessary or convenient for that purpose without further liability.

6

Sec. 3. But if said common council shall be unable to agree with the parties interested as to the damages or benefits to be assessed on account of such improvement, any judge* of the superior court, or of the supreme court of errors, may, on application of said city, after causing such notice of the pendency of such application as he shall deem just and reasonable, appoint three judicious and disinterested freeholders of the county of Hartford to estimate the damages and benefits resulting from said improvement ; and said committee, having been duly sworn, and having given notice of the time and place of their meeting for the purpose aforesaid, by publishing the same not less than twice in a newspaper published in said city, shall meet at the time and place designated, and having heard all parties in interest who shall appear before them, shall determine what parties will be damaged by said improvement in excess of special benefits, and the amount thereof ; also what parties owning or interested in lands, easements, or franchises, within a reasonable distance of· said improvement, will receive special benefit over all damage, and the amount thereof, and also what parties, if any, will receive an equal amount of damage and benefit. And thereupon said committee shall report in writing to the said judge, who may confirm, correct. or set aside said report, as he may deem just, in which latter case, said committee, or a new one to be then appointed by said judge shall proceed as before, and said report being finally accepted by said judge shall be recorded by the clerk of the superior court for Hartford county, and the award of damages and benefits therein contained shall be final between the parties ; all papers connected with said case, by whomsoever held, shall then be delivered to the clerk of the city of New Britain, who shall keep the same on file for public inspection, and said damages being paid or deposited as before provided, said city may go on to complete said public improvement and do all acts necessary or convenient for that purpose, without further liability in the premises.

Sec. 4. All amounts due to said city as special benefits under the preceding sections, whether reached by agreement or assessment, may be collected by warrant under the hand of the acting mayor of said city, directed to the collector thereof, who shall enforce the same in the same manner as tax warrants are served

---

* Amended July 1, 1873.

and enforced. Every such amount shall also be and remain a lien upon the land or other property with reference to which it was made, and said lien shall have the same validity and effect, and be enforced in the same way as provided in section thirty-seven of the act incorporating the city of New Britain. It is further provided that in no case, either of agreement or assessment, shall the aggregate amount of special benefits exceed the cost of such improvement, including damages paid and construction expenses as estimated by the committee aforesaid.

SEC. 5. This act shall be a public act, and shall take effect from and after its passage.

Approved, July 23d, 1872.

AN ACT IN ADDITION TO AN ACT INCORPORATING THE CITY OF NEW BRITAIN.

SECTION	SECTION
1. Judge of city court, disqualified or unable to act, substitute for.	2. A public act.

Be it enacted by the Senate and House of Representatives in General Assembly convened:

SECTION. 1. That in case the judge of the city court of said city of New Britain shall at any time be unable or disqualified to act in any cause, he may designate and request in writing the judge of the city court of the city of Meriden to act as his substitute ; and said judge while so acting under such request, shall have the same powers as such judge would have in like cases ; and said written request shall be recorded and kept with the records of said court by the clerk of the same.

SEC. 2. This act shall be taken to be a public act, and all acts and parts of acts inconsistent herewith are hereby repealed.

Approved, July 30th, 1872.

AN ACT IN ADDITION TO AN ACT INCORPORATING THE CITY OF NEW BRITAIN.

Be it enacted by the Senate and House of Representatives in General Assembly convened :

SECTION 1. The common council of the city of New Britain shall, as occasion may require, elect by ballot a captain and lieutenant of police, and not exceeding eight active policemen; and such other supernumerary policemen as they shall deem proper, not exceeding twenty, shall also be appointed by said common council, which officers shall hold their respective offices during good behavior, and until removed for cause. And no member of said department, now in office, or hereafter to be elected shall be removed, unless upon complaint, in writing, (a copy of which shall be furnished to him,) and after he shall have had a reasonable time, not less than six days, to prepare a defense thereto; such complaint shall be made to the common council, and may be made by any person whatsoever; *provided*, that such common·council may, by a vote of two-thirds of all the members thereof, at any regular meeting, remove or suspend for cause, any member of said department, without charges being preferred.

SEC. 2. The chief of police, the mayor, or the judge of the police court of the city, shall have power to suspend policemen from office for cause; but such suspension shall not continue for more than twenty-four hours thereafter, unless the person ordering such suspension shall within that time lodge with the clerk of the common council a notice in writing of such suspension, the ground thereof, and the names of witnesses to sustain such charges, which notice shall by said clerk be presented to the common council at the next regular meeting thereof. After notice shall have' been given to the accused, said common council, or a committee of their own number to be appointed by them, shall hear and examine witnesses under oath or affirmation upon the charges, and in defense; and said common council may continue the suspension, remove the accused from office, or return him to duty.   In all cases in which the suspension is continued, the party suspended shall be deprived of his pay from the date of his suspension, but he shall not be exempt from performance of duty, unless the officer making such suspension shall so expressly order.   The violation of any law of the state, or ordinance of the city, or of any rule or regulation of the police department, or incompetency, shall, if proved, be punished by suspension or dismissal from the force.

SEC. 3.   In case either of said offices shall at any time become vacant by reason of death or otherwise, said common council may fill any such vacancy; and any person chosen to fill such vacancy shall hold said office during good behavior, subject to be removed for cause, or suspended, as aforesaid.

SEC. 4.   The mayor of said city of New Britain, shall, by and with the advice and consent of the aldermen thereof, within one month after this act shall take effect, appoint six freeholders of said city, who shall not be members of the common council, and who shall constitute a board of street commissioners of said city: and the appointment of the members of said board shall be made in such a manner as to divide the membership thereof as nearly as may be, equally, between the two leading political parties for the time being.   The persons so appointed shall hold their office, two for the term of one year; two for the term of two years, and two for the term of three years, from and after the third Wednesday of April, 1873, which terms shall be designated by the mayor at the time of making the appointments aforesaid.   During the month of April, 1874, and annually thereafter, during said month, the mayor and aldermen of said city shall appoint two members of said board, who shall hold office for the term of three years, from the third Wednesday of April of the year in which they are so elected, and until their respective successors shall be appointed and qualified, and in such appointment regard shall be had for the two leading political parties for the time being, as aforesaid.

SEC. 5.   Said board of street commissioners shall act as a court, for the assessment of betterments and appraisal of damages, and all powers now conferred by the charter of the city of New Britain in reference to the appraisal of damages and assessment of betterments, shall hereafter be exercised by said board: *provided* the common council shall have power to pass ordinances not inconsistent herewith, prescribing the manner of procedure in such assessment and appraisal.

SEC. 6.   The members of said board shall be sworn by the clerk of said city to a faithful and impartial discharge of their duties, and a certificate of such appointment, and the administration of such oath, shall be made and recorded in the records of the city.

SEC. 7.   Whenever a vacancy shall occur in said board of street commissioners, it shall be filled in the manner provided aforesaid for the appointment of members.

SEC. 8.   The mayor of said city, by and with the advice of any two of the aldermen, may remove any member of said board for cause.

SEC. 9.   In all cases when it becomes necessary to estimate and appraise the damages or benefits, as the case may be, resulting or accruing to any person or persons from the taking of land or any interest therein, for public use, or from the laying out, alteration, construction, extension, enlargement, discontinuance, or exchange of any street, highway, public walk, sewer, or avenue, or designation of any building line or lines, as provided in the charter of said city of New Britain, or whenever the common council shall order the paving of any street or highway, or any part thereof, the board of street commissioners shall obtain from the city surveyor a map, drawing, or written description, clearly explaining the contemplated improvement, and showing the adjoining land and owners thereof, and shall then agree, if possible, with persons owning or interested in lands required for said improvement, upon the compensation to be made therefor, including the damages for establishing a building line or lines in case of opening a new street, and with those who will be specially benefited by said improvement as to the entire amount to be paid as betterments for said improvement, and the respective amounts or proportions thereof, which each person so benefited will pay, and secure from each such owner or person, proper written evidence of such agreement.

SEC. 10.   If said board of street commissioners fail to agree with any owner of said land or interest therein, or with any of the parties, who, in their opinion, should be assessed for any benefits on account of said proposed improvement, they shall, before making any assessment of damages and benefits, give reasonable notice to all persons interested in said proposed improvement, of the time and place when and where they will meet for that purpose; such notice shall be deemed reasonable and sufficient, if signed by the members of said board, or a majority of them, and published in the same manner as provided to be done by the common council in section thirty-five of said charter, or if given in such other manner as by an ordinance of the common council is now or may be prescribed; said board shall meet at the time and place designated in their said notice, and at such other times and places as they may adjourn therefrom, and all parties in interest may appear before said commissioners and be heard with witnesses relative to the amount of damages or betterments, or both, to be appraised or assessed to them respectively, and said commissioners shall examine said parties and witnesses under oath; thereupon said board shall proceed to assess all betterments or benefits, and to appraise all damages therefor, to the persons liable to such betterments, or entitled to such damages, including the damages for building lines in case of new streets, or alteration of existing streets, upon the proper parties or land specially benefited by said proposed improvement, in proportion to the benefits or damages to each respectively: *provided*, that the whole amount of benefits assessed for any particular lay-out, alteration, designation, or other improvement, shall not exceed the whole amount of damages assessed on account of the same lay-out, alteration, designation, or improvement, and the estimated cost of constructing and completing said improvement, which estimate said board shall make and take into consideration in their assessments as provided in this section, and their attempts to agree with the parties in interest as to betterments as aforesaid, and shall also embody in the report of their doings, which report shall be made as soon as may be, to the common council of said city; and all the subsequent proceedings relative to said assessment, shall be the same as is now provided in said charter, except as the same is hereinafter altered, in regard to appeals; and the assessment of betterments shall be and remain a lien or real incumbrance upon the land upon which they are respectively made as is now provided.

SEC. 11. All appeals taken from any appraisal of damage or

assessment of betterments, made by the board of street commissioners of said city, shall be to the judge of the court of common pleas for the county of Hartford; and, when an appeal shall be taken, said board shall instruct and aid the city attorney in the matter of said appeal, until the same shall be determined. As many of the parties interested as may choose to do so may join in such appeal; and when separate appeals are taken by different parties from one assessment and appraisal, all such appeals shall be heard and tried as one cause.*

SEC. 12. Appeals may be taken from the assessment of benefits only; but, if taken from the appraisal of damages, shall be from the said appraisal and also from the assessment of benefits made at the same time and for the same, public work. Such appeal shall be taken within ten days after public notice shall be given of such appraisal or assessment, and shall be by a suitable petition in writing, setting forth the whole of said assessment appealed from, and asking for a re-appraisal and re-assessment, or for a re-assessment only, with a citation attached thereto, signed by any authority authorized to sign writs, returnable before said judge at 2 o'clock, P. M., on the day three weeks subsequent to the day on which public notice of said appraisal shall have been given; and said citation shall be served upon the clerk of said city at least six days before the return day thereof.

SEC. 13. Such appeals may be heard by said judge, but shall, upon the motion of any party thereto, or person interested therein, be referred to a committee for hearing.

SEC. 14. If, upon the hearing of any appeal, said judge or committee shall find cause to alter said assessment, or said appraisal and assessment, then said judge or committee shall proceed to re-assess the whole amount of the damages or cost of construction, or both, upon the persons or land specially benefited.

SEC. 15. If the judge or committee hearing said appeal, shall alter said assessment or said appraisal and assessment, as aforesaid, then said·judge or committee shall cause notice of the pendency of the proceedings before him, to be given to all persons interested in said proposed improvement, which notice shall be by citation, served upon such persons, or left at their usual place of abode, giving such time for appearance, and served in such manner, as

---

* See act of June 18, 1875, relating to appeals and assessments.

said court or committee shall direct, or by publication in a newspaper published in said city, for such time and in such form as said judge or committee shall direct.

SEC. 16. Such judge shall have, for the purpose of disposing of said appeal, all the power of the superior court, and may render judgment thereon, and may tax costs in favor of either party, and issue execution for said costs, to be taxed as upon civil process in the superior court.

SEC. 17. Said judge shall, when the proceedings in any case arising under this act are closed, return all papers connected with the case to the clerk of said city, to be by him kept on file.

SEC. 18. Section seventy of the act to which this act is an addition, is hereby amended by striking out the word "Monday," in the second line of said section, and inserting, in place thereof, the word "Wednesday."

SEC. 19. This act shall be a public act, and shall take effect from its passage, and all acts and parts of acts, and ordinances and parts of ordinances, inconsistent herewith, are hereby repealed: *provided*, that An Act in addition to an Act incorporating the City of New Britain, passed at the May session, A. D. 1872, and approved July 23d of the same year, shall remain in full force and effect the same as if this act had not been passed, and that this act shall not affect any suit now pending.

Approved, July 1st, 1873.

AN ACT IN ADDITION TO AN ACT INCORPORATING THE CITY OF NEW BRITAIN.

Be it enacted by the Senate and House of Representatives in General Assembly convened:

SECTION 1. That for the purposes of defraying the cost and expense incident to the laying out, construction and repairing of sewers and drains in the city of New Britain, and of paying the indebtedness of said city already accrued, and now existing on

7

account of the purchase of the "Shepard property," so-called, and for said purposes only, the said city of New Britain is hereby authorized and empowered to issue notes, scrip, or certificates of debt, to be denominated on the face thereof, the sewer fund of the city of New Britain, to an amount not exceeding in the whole the sum of one hundred and fifty thousand ($150,000) dollars, bearing interest at no greater rate than   per cent. per annum, the principal of which shall be payable at some certain time or times within   years from issuing the same, and the amount of said notes, scrip, or certificates which may at any time be issued, together with the times of payment of the principal and interest thereof, and the rate of interest shall be prescribed by said city in legal meeting for that purpose called and held, and said notes, scrip, or certificates shall be signed by the mayor and countersigned by the treasurer of said city, and shall, when issued, be obligatory on said city and the inhabitants thereof, according to the tenor of the same, and all sums of money realized from the sale or other disposition of said "Shepard property," or any portion thereof, or from sewer assessments, shall belong to the sewer fund of said city, and shall be used for sewer purposes only; no assessment of benefits for sewer purposes shall be collectible until the completion of the sewer for which the party or parties are assessed.

SEC. 2. The common council of said city shall, within one month after the acceptance of the provisions of this act by the city as hereinafter provided, proceed to appoint three persons, who may or may not be members of said common council, who shall act as a board of sewer commissioners, with the powers conferred by this act, and the persons so appointed shall hold their office, one for the term of one year, one for the term of two years, and one for the term of three years, from and after the third Wednesday of April, 1874, which terms shall be designated by the common council at the time of making the appointment. During the month of April, 1875, and annually thereafter during said month, the common council of said city shall appoint one member of said board, who shall hold office for the term of three years from the third Wednesday of April of the year in which he is so appointed, and until his successor shall be appointed and qualified.

SEC. 3. Said board of sewer commissioners shall be the trustees of the notes, scrip, or certificates of debt issued by said city under the provisions of this act, shall superintend the issuing of the same and regulate the particular form thereof, and after the same or any part thereof shall be issued, they may sell the same in such manner and on such terms as they may deem best, or they may pledge the same for moneys borrowed by said city to be used for sewer purposes. Said board shall keep a record of all such notes, scrip, or certificates issued, disposed of or pledged, and all moneys received by said board shall be by them paid over to the treasurer of said city.

Sec. 4. Said board of sewer commissioners are authorized and empowered to attend to the construction. supervision, care, and management of the sewers and drains of said city. and to exercise any additional powers conferred upon them by said common council, and they shall keep a record of their official proceedings, and shall render a report of their doings to said common council annually, and oftener when by them requested, including a general exhibit of the state of their works, on account of sums required to be expended therefor, and such other matters of information as may be called for by said common council: *provided*, that said board shall always be under the direction of the common council of said city. and none of the powers heretofore by law vested in said council shall be divested by this act.

Sec. 5. This act shall take effect from its passage, and when approved by a majority of the legal voters of said city, present at a meeting duly warned and held for that purpose.

Approved, June 9th, 1874.

AN ACT AMENDING AN ACT INCORPORATING THE CITY OF NEW BRITAIN.

Be it enacted by the Senate and House of Representatives in General Assembly convened:

Section 1. The city of New Britain shall be divided into four wards designated and bounded as follows, to wit: So much of said city as lies southerly and westerly of a line commencing at the western limit of said city, and in the center of West Main street, so called; thence easterly on the center line of said West Main street to the center line of Main street; thence southerly on the center line of said Main street to South Main street; thence on the center line of said South Main street, to the southern limit of said city, shall constitute and remain the first ward. So much of said city as lies easterly and southerly of a line commencing at the southern limit of said city, and in the center of South Main street; running thence in the easterly boundary of said first ward, and continuing on the center line of said Main street to the center line of the Hartford, Providence and Fishkill railroad track; thence easterly, on the center line of said railroad track, to East Main street; thence on the center line of said East Main street, to the eastern limit of said city, shall constitute and remain the second ward. So much of said city as lies northerly and westerly of a line commencing at the same point in the western limit of said city, heretofore described as the point where the boundary of the first ward commences; running thence in the northerly boundary of said first ward to the center of Main street; thence northerly on the center line of said Main street, and running east of Liberty Square, so called, to the center line of Sexton street; thence on the center line of said Sexton street to the northern limit of said city, shall constitute and remain the third ward. So much of said city as lies easterly and northerly of a line commencing at the northern limit of said city, and in the center of Sexton street; running thence in the eastern boundary of said third ward to the center of the Hartford, Providence and Fishkill railroad track; thence in the northern boundary of said second ward to the eastern limit of said city, shall constitute and remain the fourth ward.

SEC. 2.   Section four of the act to which this act is an amendment, is hereby amended by striking out the word, "six," in the fifth line of said section, and inserting in lieu thereof the word "four."

SEC. 3.   Whenever a vote, resolution, order, or ordinance, passed by the common council of said city, shall have been disapproved by the mayor, and by him returned to the common council, with his objections thereto in writing, if two-thirds of all the members of said common council, present and absent, shall vote to pass such resolution, vote, order, or ordinance, notwithstanding the mayor's objections, the same shall be valid as if it had been approved by the mayor, but not otherwise.

SEC. 4. Whenever a sidewalk has been laid by an adjoining land-owner, under any order of the common council of said city, and upon a grade furnished by competent city authority, and it is deemed necessary by said common council, at any time within ten years thereafter, to alter or change such grade and relay such side-walk, such alteration or change of grade and relaying of sidewalk shall be done at the expense of said city: *provided*, that in all cases where an alteration or change of grade, or the relaying of any sidewalk is made necessary by an alteration or exchange of any street line, the expense thereof shall be chargeable as is now pro-vided by law. The provisions of this section shall extend and apply to sidewalks already formed, and flagged or paved in com-pliance with the orders of the common council.

SEC. 5. The common council of said city shall annually, in the month of March, and on or before the twenty-fifth day of that month, make a detailed estimate of the expenses of said city, and of each department thereof, during the year ending on the fifteenth day of April next following, and cause the same to be published in each of the newspapers of said city. The said estimates, with such explanations and suggestions as the said common council shall deem proper to submit, shall be submitted to the next annual meet-ing of said city, and shall be considered and acted upon at an ad-journed meeting, to be held within ten days after the time appointed for the said annual meeting. If the said meeting approve of the said estimates, they shall authorize the requisite appropriations to be made by the said common council to pay the amount thereof; but if they disapprove of the said estimates, or any of them, they shall make such alterations therein as they shall judge proper, and shall authorize the appropriations required to pay the sums called for by said estimates so altered by them. And it shall not be law-ful for the said common council to make appropriations from the city treasury, or in any manner bind said city for a sum in excess of the estimates so approved or altered by said meeting, without the sanction of the voters of said city. A tax shall be laid at said adjourned annual meeting to meet the appropriation voted, and any additional sum voted at any special meeting of said city, shall also be provided for by a tax laid at said special meeting. The mayor or other executive officer shall be held personally liable for the amount of any order drawn, or obligation given, in violation of this section.

Sec. 6. No expenditure of money for the year ending on the fifteenth day of May, 1875, in excess of the amount covered by the tax now laid, shall be made by said common council until authorized by a major vote of a city meeting legally warned and held for that purpose, and a special tax laid to meet such appropriation.

Sec. 7. This act shall be a public act, and all acts and parts of acts, and ordinances and parts of ordinances, which may be inconsistent herewith, are hereby repealed.

Approved, June 17th, 1874.

AN ACT AMENDING AN ACT INCORPORATING THE CITY OF NEW BRITAIN.

Section	Section
1. Water Commissioners.	2. Repeals in part section seventy-five of charter.

Be it enacted by the Senate and House of Representatives in General Assembly convened:

Section 1. The common council of the city of New Britain shall, within twenty days after the passage of this act, choose by ballot three water commissioners, who shall be residents of said city, and in voting for such commissioners each member of said council shall vote for three persons, whose names shall be written or printed on one ballot, and shall be marked and designated respectively, as first, second, and third. The person receiving a majority of the votes marked first, shall be declared to be elected for one year, and until another is duly chosen in his place ; the person receiving a majority of the votes marked second, shall be declared to be elected for two years, and until another is chosen in his place ; and the person receiving a majority of the votes marked third, shall be declared to be elected for three years, and until another is chosen in his stead. And said common council shall annually thereafter, in the month of May, choose by ballot, one resident of said city to serve as water commissioner for the term of three years, and until another is chosen in his place ; the person receiving a majority of the votes to be declared elected.

Said common council shall, in the same manner, fill any vacancies which may occur in said board.

Sec. 2.   This act shall take effect from its passage, and so much of section seventy-five of the charter of the city of New Britain as is inconsistent herewith, is hereby repealed.

Approved, May 26th, 1875.

AN ACT IN ADDITION TO AN ACT INCORPORATING THE CITY OF NEW BRITAIN.

Be it enacted by the Senate and House of Representatives in General Assembly convened:

SECTION 1.   That upon the execution of any order of the common council of said city for the construction of any lateral branch, or connecting public sewer, there may be assessed by the board of street commissioners of said city, upon all persons whose property is, in the judgment of said board, especially benefited thereby, a reasonable part of the expense of such lateral branch or connecting public sewer, and of the main or trunk sewer into and through which such lateral branch or connecting sewer is discharged : *always provided*, that no person shall be assessed for sewer purposes under this act, or the act to which it is amendatory, beyond the amount to which his property is especially benefited, whether the property on account of which such assessments are made, be located along the line of a main or trunk sewer, or of a lateral branch, or connecting sewer.

Sec. 2.   No person owning land fronting on the line of a street in which a sewer is constructed, shall be assessed more than one dollar and twenty-five cents per foot front of said land, unless in the opinion of said street commissioners the owner thereof is the own-er of land in the rear that will be specially benefited by said sewer.   No assessment of benefits shall be made until the sewer, on which assessments are based, shall be placed under contract, or be collectible before completion of said sewer.

SEC. 3. This act shall apply to all assessments hereafter to be made on account of sewers now or hereafter completed.

SEC. 4. That the time of opening the police court of said city shall be eight o'clock in the forenoon, instead of nine, as is now provided.

SEC. 5. This act shall be a public act and shall take effect from its passage.

Approved, June 24th, 1875.

AN ACT AMENDING THE CHARTER OF THE CITY OF NEW BRITAIN, AND FIXING THE SALARY OF THE JUDGE OF THE CITY COURT.

SECTION	SECTION
1. Salary of Judge of City Court.	2. Repeals previous acts.

Be it enacted by the Senate and House of Representatives in General Assembly convened :

SECTION 1. The salary of the judge of the city court of the city of New Britain, from and after the fourth day of July, A. D. 1875. shall be the sum of eight hundred dollars per annum.

SEC. 2. All acts or parts of acts inconsistent herewith, are hereby repealed.

Approved, July 2d. 1875.

AN ACT AMENDING THE CHARTER OF THE CITY OF NEW BRITAIN.

SECTION	SECTION
1. Jurisdiction of police court extended over Shuttle Meadow lake.	3. Jurisdiction of officers of town of Southington.
2. Town, city, and police officers empowered to make arrests at.	4. A public act.

Be it enacted by the Senate and House of Representatives in General Assembly convened :

SECTION 1. The police court of the city of New Britain shall have jurisdiction over all crimes, offenses, and misdemeanors that shall be committed in that part of the town of Southington, in the county of Hartford, covered by the waters of the Shuttle Meadow lake, so called, and within one hundred rods, measuring landward, from the high water line of said lake along the entire border thereof, in the same manner as said court now has over crimes, offenses, and misdemeanors that are committed within the limits of the town and city of New Britain.

SEC. 2.   The officers of the town and of the city of New Britain, and members of the police department of said city, shall have the same authority and power to arrest any person, or persons within that part of the town of Southington described in section first of this act, as they now have to make arrests within the limits of the town and city of New Britain, and all persons so arrested by them shall be brought forthwith before the police court of said city, which court shall thereupon proceed to trial and judgment as in all other similar cases now within its jurisdiction.

SEC. 3.   Nothing in this act contained shall affect the jurisdiction of grand jurors, or other informing officers of the town of Southington, or of justices of the peace of said town over crimes, offenses, and misdemeanors committed in any part of said town of Southington.

SEC. 4.   This act shall be a public act, and shall take effect from its passage.

Approved, July 20th, 1875.

AN ACT AMENDING AN ACT INCORPORATING THE CITY OF NEW BRITAIN.

SECTION	SECTION
1. Registry lists of wards.	4. Annual report of mayor and treasurer.
2. Jurisdiction of city court.	5. A public act.
3. Building and alteration of buildings.	

Be it enacted by the Senate and House of Representatives in General Assembly convened:

SECTION 1.   Whenever any annual meeting for the choice of city officers, or any meeting where a vote is to be taken by ballot, in the wards of said city, is to be held, the registrars whose duty it is to prepare the registry list or lists, for electors' meetings in

8

the town of New Britain, shall prepare a list as nearly perfect as is practicable, of the names of the persons entitled to vote in each and every ward of said city, at the said city meeting, and of the street in which each person resides, and whenever the residence of such person is numbered, the number thereof, which names shall be arranged in alphabetical order, for which services said registrars shall be paid a reasonable compensation from the city treasury, not exceeding two hundred dollars each ; said list or lists shall be delivered by said registrars to the city clerk at least three days prior to such meeting, and shall be open to the inspection of any elector of said city. The presiding officer of every ward meeting may receive the votes of all persons whose names are on the ward list prepared as aforesaid, unless the right of any such person to vote at such ward meeting is challenged, in which case said presiding officer shall, before receiving such vote, if requested by the challenger, make due inquiry into the right of such person to vote, and hear and determine such challenge, and if of the opinion that such person is legally entitled to vote at such ward meeting, the presiding officer shall receive his vote ; otherwise he shall reject his vote. In case any person whose name is not on such ward voting list shall offer to vote at said meeting, the presiding officer of such ward meeting shall proceed to inquire into the right of such person to vote, and if of the opinion that such person is legally entitled to vote in said ward meeting, shall cause the name and residence of such person to be entered on such ward voting list, and receive his vote ; otherwise he shall reject the same. Every person who shall be examined by any presiding officer relative to the right of himself or any other person to vote, shall be under oath, which oath the presiding officer shall administer ; and, if any person when so examined shall be guilty of willful false swearing, he shall be liable to the penalties of perjury.

Sec. 2. That "An act incorporating the city of New Britain," passed by the general assembly of this state at the May session thereof, A. D. 1870, and approved July 15, 1870, be amended by striking out all after the word "have" in the sixth line, and before the word "The" in the twenty-fifth line of the fortieth section, and inserting in lieu thereof, the following, viz : "Jurisdiction in all civil causes, and over all suits in equity (excepting suits for relief against any cause depending or judgment rendered in the superior court or court of common pleas), which shall be brought before it according to law, in which the debt, damages, or matter in demand exceeds the jurisdiction of a justice of the peace, and does not exceed the sum of five hundred dollars : *provided*, the cause of the proceedings in equity originated, and one or both of the parties reside within the limits of said town of New Britain, and the premises in question, in cases of foreclosure or other proceedings relating to real estate, shall be situated in said town ; and in all cases in which the matter in demand shall exceed the sum of three hundred dollars, an appeal from any final judgment rendered thereon, shall be had and allowed to either party, upon giving bond with surety to the satisfaction of the judge of said court, to the next superior court of the county of Hartford." But this amendment shall not prevent said court from proceeding to hear and determine any action now. pending before it, in which the matter in demand exceeds the sum of five hundred dollars.

SEC. 3. That said "act incorporating the city of New Britain " be further amended by inserting in line fourteen of the twenty-second section thereof, after the words "by fire " and before the words "the markets," the following : "and for that purpose, and to provide for the greater safety of occupants of buildings from fire, to. regulate the alteration of buildings, and the mode of building, and the materials used for building or altering buildings, and the mode of using buildings."

SEC. 4. That said "act incorporating the city of New Britain " be further amended by inserting the word "April " in the place of the word "March," in the thirty-fifth line of the tenth section of said act, and by inserting the word "April " in the place of the word "March," in the fourth line of the sixteenth section of said act, and by inserting the word "March " in the place of the word "February," in the seventh line of said sixteenth section.

SEC. 5. This act shall be a public act, and shall take effect from its passage, and all acts and parts of acts inconsistent herewith are hereby repealed.

Approved, June 19th, 1876.

CHARTER

OF THE

WATER-WORKS,

ACCEPTED JUNE 4, 1857,

AND AMENDMENTS.

ACTS AUTHORIZING THE ISSUE OF WATER BONDS,

AND

ACT RELATING TO APPEALS AND ASSESSMENTS.

WATER-WORKS.

AN ACT TO SUPPLY THE BOROUGH OF NEW BRITAIN WITH WATER FOR PUBLIC AND PRIVATE PURPOSES.

Be it enacted by the Senate and House of Representatives in General Assembly convened:

SECTION 1. That *" the borough of New Britain," is hereby authorized and empowered to take water from the stream known as "Shuttle Meadow Brook," at any feasible point near the southwest corner of the town of New Britain, either within or without the limits of said town; provided that rights of other proprietors sustaining damage thereby, be paid for by said borough, as hereinafter provided, and such water to convey and distribute into and through the said borough, by means of aqueducts, reservoirs, and other suitable works, in such quantities as the necessities and conveniences of said borough may require; also, to take and hold any lands or other estate, or any privileges, and to exercise any powers not inconsistent with the laws of this state, that may be necessary or convenient for carrying into full effect the purposes of this act.†

SEC. 2. Said borough shall immediately upon its acceptance of the provisions of this act, proceed to elect three persons, who shall act as a board of water commissioners, with the powers con-

---

* See amendment next following. † Amended, May 30, 1860.

ferred by this act, and shall hold office until the next annual meeting of said borough, and until others are chosen in their stead and sworn, and at each annual meeting hereafter there shall be chosen three water commissioners, to hold office for one year, and until their successors are sworn.*

SEC. 3.   Said commissioners are hereby authorized and empowered to purchase and take conveyances for and in the name of the borough, of all lands, or other estates or privileges, necessary or convenient for accomplishing the purposes of this act; to make contracts for labor and materials for the general purposes contemplated by this act; to dam and hold in sufficient quantities the water of said stream; to lay and construct all necessary pipes, aqueducts, or reservoirs, either within or without said borough; to make use of the ground or soil under any railroad, street, high or private way, for the purposes of laying said pipes or aqueducts in such manner as least to obstruct or impede travel thereon, causing all damage done thereto to be repaired, and all damages sustained by any person or corporation, in consequence of the interruption of travel, to be paid to such person or corporation; to make and establish public reservoirs and hydrants, under the direction of the warden and burgesses; to regulate the distribution and use of said water, and establish the prices to be paid therefor. *Provided*, that in the regulation of said water for all public uses, said board shall be under the direction of the warden and burgesses; to collect all water rents, and pay over the same to the borough treasurer, to audit, allow, and draw orders on the treasurer for the payment of all claims against said borough on account of said water-works, and generally to attend to the construction, supervision, care and management of said water-works, and to exercise any additional powers that may from time to time be conferred upon them by said borough; and they shall keep a record of their official proceedings and render a report of their doings to said borough, including a general exhibit of the state of the works, an account of sums required to be expended therefor, and such other matters of information as may be called for by the warden and burgesses at each annual meeting; and to the warden and burgesses whenever by them required; and said commissioner shall keep regular books of account.

SEC. 4.   A majority of said commissioners shall constitute a quorum for the transaction of any of the business of said board, and all vacancies which shall occur in said board, by death, resig-

---

* See Sec. 75 city charter, and amendment thereto May 26. 1875.

nation, or otherwise, shall be filled as soon as may be by the warden and burgesses.

SEC. 5. Whenever disagreement shall be had between said board and the owner or owners of any property or privileges which may be required for the purposes of this act, as to the amount of compensation or damages to be paid to such owner or owners for the same, or whenever such owner shall by law be incapable of contracting, or be absent from this state, such compensation or damages may be assessed by three disinterested persons, under oath, appointed by either judge of the supreme court of errors, on application made to said judge, by or on behalf of either party, after such notice shall be given of such application, as said judge shall see fit to prescribe, which said appraisers shall report their doings, embracing the amount of their assessment, to the clerk of the superior court for Hartford county, to be by him recorded, and thereupon such assessment shall be taken and held to be a final adjustment of said compensation and damages between said parties, and upon payment thereof, or deposit of the same with the county treasurer, to the use of such owner or owners, said commissioners may proceed with the construction of said works, without liability to any further claim to compensation or damages.

SEC. 6. For the purpose of defraying the cost of construction of said water-works, including the cost of purchase and the other expenses incident thereto, and for no other purpose whatever, said borough is hereby authorized and empowered to issue notes, scrip, or certificates of debt, to be denominated on the face thereof, "Water Fund of the borough of New Britain," to an amount not exceeding in the whole the sum of fifty thousand dollars, bearing interest at no greater rate than seven per cent. per annum, the principal of which shall be payable at some certain time or times, within thirty years from issuing of the same, and the amount of said notes, scrip, or certificates which may at any time be issued together with the times of payment of the principal and interest thereof, and the rate of interest shall be prescribed by said borough, in legal borough meeting for that purpose specially called and held, and said notes, scrip, or certificates shall be signed by the warden and countersigned by the treasurer of said borough, and shall, when issued, be obligatory upon said borough and the inhabitants thereof, according to the purport and tenor of the same.

Sec. 7.   Said board of water commissioners shall be the trustees of the notes, scrip, or certificates of debt, issued by said borough, shall superintend the issuing of the same, and regulate the particular form thereof, and after the same or any part thereof shall be issued, they may sell the same, in such manner and on such terms as they may deem best, or they may pledge the same for moneys borrowed by said borough, to be used in or about the construction of said works.   And said board shall keep a record of all such notes, scrip, or certificates issued, disposed of, or pledged, and all moneys received by said board shall be by them paid over to the borough treasurer.

Sec. 8.   The avails of all water rents shall be first applied to defraying the ordinary and current expenses of said water-works, after which, to the payment of the interest on said notes, scrip, or certificates, and if there shall at any time still be an excess, the borough treasurer shall report the fact to the warden and burgesses, who may direct whether the same be applied to the extinguishment of the principal debt incurred by the issuing of said notes, scrip, or certificates, or to any other purpose in connection with said works.

Sec. 9.   In case the avails of water rents in any year shall be inadequate to meet the current expenses of said water-works, and the interest of said notes, scrip, or certificates, the deficiency shall be supplied by the laying of a tax on the grand list of all persons liable to borough taxation, which said tax may be laid at any borough meeting legally called for that purpose, and said borough may at any borough meeting for that purpose specially called and held, lay taxes for the purpose of paying the principal debt aforesaid, or any part thereof, by the establishment of a sinking fund or in any other manner.

Sec. 10.   Taxes laid for the purposes mentioned in the preceding section, may be collected in the same manner as other borough taxes, and any claim of said borough for the use of water, shall be a lien upon the house, tenement, or lot, wherein, or in connection with which, said water was used by the owner or occupier thereof.   And said lien may be foreclosed before any court having jurisdiction, in the same manner as a mortgage is now foreclosed, according to the rules of equity.

Sec. 11.   It shall be the duty of said commissioners to designate in all orders by them drawn upon the treasurer, the class to which the same belongs, whether construction account or expense account, and the treasurer shall pay all such orders from the appro-, priate fund as established in the foregoing sections of this act. And such commissioners and treasurer shall give bonds with sufficient surety for the faithful performance of their several trusts in such sums and shall receive for their services such compensations as the warden and burgesses shall prescribe.

SEC. 12. If any person shall willfully and maliciously corrupt the water in any reservoir, hydrant, aqueduct pipe or other portion of said water-works, or destroy or injure any portion of such works, or any materials or property used or designed to be used in connection therewith, he shall forfeit and pay to said borough treble damages in an action of trespass brought by said borough, and such person, on conviction thereof before any court having jurisdiction of the offense, shall be punished by fine not exceeding three hundred dollars, or by imprisonment not exceeding one year, or by such fine and imprisonment both.

SEC. 13. This act shall to all intents and purposes be a public act, and may be altered, amended, or repealed by the general assembly; and the same shall not go into effect until it has been accepted by said borough at a borough meeting legally warned for that purpose, in conformity with the provisions of the by-laws of said borough for the warning of special meetings thereof, and to be held within two weeks from the date of the passage hereof, at which meeting the votes shall be taken by ballots, written "yes" and "no," and if two-thirds of the ballots so cast in said meeting shall have upon the same the word "yes," then this act shall be in full force, otherwise the same shall be null and void; the boxes to receive the ballots aforesaid shall be kept open on such day of voting from nine o'clock A. M., until two o'clock P. M., and the votes shall be counted and the result declared in the manner prescribed for the election of the annual officers of said borough; and if at said meeting this act shall be accepted by said borough, said borough may thereupon proceed at the same meeting to vote upon the matter of issuing said notes, scrip, or certificates, and to elect said commissioners and transact any other business contemplated in the provisions of this act, provided notice thereof shall have been inserted in the call for said meeting.

SEC. 14. This act shall take effect from the day of its acceptance, in manner aforesaid, by the said borough of New Britain.

AN ACT IN AMENDMENT OF AN ACT ENTITLED "AN ACT TO SUPPLY THE BOROUGH OF NEW BRITAIN WITH WATER FOR PUBLIC AND PRIVATE PURPOSES."

Be it enacted by the Senate and House of Representatives in General Assembly convened:

SECTION 1. That the act entitled "An act to supply the borough of New Britain with water for public and private purposes," passed at this session of the general assembly, be amended by the insertion of the words, "The warden, burgesses, and freemen of," between the words "that" and "the" in the first line of the first section of said act.

SEC. 2. This act shall be a public act, and take effect from its its passage.

AMENDING "AN ACT TO SUPPLY THE BOROUGH OF NEW BRITAIN WITH WATER FOR PUBLIC AND PRIVATE PURPOSES."

SECTION
1. Extension of water pipes to town limits authorized.

SECTION
2. When act takes effect.

Resolved by this Assembly:

SECTION 1. That the warden, burgesses, and freemen of the borough of New Britain be, and they hereby are, authorized and empowered to extend and continue their water pipes to localities without the limits of said borough, and within the town of New Britain, and to supply and distribute water by them taken under the provision of said act, to the proprietors or occupants of such localities, upon such terms as may be agreed upon between said proprietors or occupants and the proper officers of said borough; and all the powers and privileges conferred upon said borough by said act, shall apply to this act, so far as may be necessary to make the same fully effectual for the purposes aforesaid; *provided*, that this act may be altered, amended, or repealed at the pleasure of the general assembly.

SEC. 2. This act shall take effect from the day of its passage.
Approved, May 30th, 1860.

AUTHORIZING THE BOROUGH OF NEW BRITAIN TO ISSUE BONDS FOR PROCURING AN ADDITIONAL SUPPLY OF WATER.

Resolved by this Assembly :

That the warden, burgesses, and freemen of the borough of New Britain are hereby authorized to take and hold any and all lands and other estate that may be necessary for laying an additional pipe from the present reservoir of the water works to the said borough, said land and other estate to be taken, held and compensation to be made in the manner provided in the "Act to supply the borough of New Britain with water for public and private purposes."

Resolved further, That for the purpose of defraying the cost of laying such additional main pipe, and other expenses incident to the construction and completion of said water works, and for said purpose only, said borough is hereby authorized and empowered to issue notes, scrip or certificates of debt, to be denominated on the face thereof, the "Water Fund of the Borough of New Britain, second series," to an amount not exceeding in the whole the sum of seventy-five thousand dollars, bearing interest at no greater rate than seven per cent. per annum, the principal of which shall be payable at some certain time or times within thirty years from issuing the same, and the amount of said notes, scrip, or certificates which may at any time be issued, together with the times of payment of the principal and interest thereof, and the rate of interest shall be prescribed by said borough in legal meeting for that purpose called and held, and said notes, scrip or certificates shall be signed by the warden and countersigned by the treasurer of said borough, and shall, when issued, be obligatory upon said borough and the inhabitants thereof according to the tenor of the same ; and the water commissioners of said borough shall have the same interest in, and power over said bonds for the purposes aforesaid, which they now have by law in and over bonds hitherto issued pursuant to the charter of said water-works: *provided*, that this act shall not take effect, until approved by a majority of the legal voters of said borough, at a meeting duly warned and held for that purpose.

Approved, July 11th, 1867.

AUTHORIZING THE ISSUE OF BALANCE OF BONDS HERETO-FORE AUTHORIZED BY THE BOROUGH OF NEW BRITAIN BY THE CITY OF NEW BRITAIN.

Whereas, the general assembly of the state of Connecticut, at the May session thereof, in the year 1867, did pass a resolution authorizing the community, then known as the warden, bur-gesses, and freemen of the borough of New Britain, to issue notes, scrip, or certificates of debt, to the amount of seventy-five thousand dollars for the purposes of aiding in the construc-tion and completion of the water works of said New Britain: and whereas, said community did accept said resolution, as provided therein, and has duly issued bonds pursuant thereto, to the amount of fifty thousand dollars : and whereas said com-munity, now known as the city of New Britain is desirous of issuing the amount of bonds remaining to be issued, under the original grant of authority aforesaid,

Resolved by this Assembly:

That said city of New Britain is hereby authorized to issue its notes, scrip, or certificates of debt to the amount of twenty-five thousand dollars, to be denominated on the face thereof the Water Fund of the City of New Britain, and to be signed by the mayor and countersigned by the treasurer of said city, but to be in all other respects conformatory to the provisions of the orig-inal resolution accepted as aforesaid.

Approved, June 16th, 1871.

AUTHORIZING THE CITY OF NEW BRITAIN TO ISSUE ADDI-TIONAL WATER BONDS.

Resolved by this Assembly :

That for the purpose of defraying the cost and expenses inci-dent to the construction, completion, and extension of the water-works of the city of New Britain, and for said purpose only, the said city of New Britain is hereby authorized and empowered to issue notes, scrip, or certificates of debt, to be denominated on the face thereof, the Water Fund of the City of New Britain, third series, to an amount not exceeding, in the whole, the sum of seventy-five thousand dollars, ($75,000,) bearing interest at no greater rate than seven per cent. per annum, the principal of which shall be payable at some certain time or times within thirty years from issuing the same, and the amount of said notes, scrip, or certificates, which may at any time be issued, together with the times of payment of the principal and interest thereof ; and the rate of interest shall be prescribed by said city, in legal meeting for that purpose called and held, and said notes, scrip, or certificates, shall be signed by the mayor, and counter-signed by the treasurer of said city, and shall, when issued, be obligatory on said city and the inhabitants thereof, according to the tenor of the same ; and the water commissioners of said city shall have the same interest in and power over said bonds for the purposes aforesaid, which they now have, by law, over the bonds commonly known as "water bonds," hitherto issued by the borough and the city of New Britain, under the various acts authorizing the same : *provided*, that this act shall not take effect until approved by a majority of the legal voters of said city, at a meeting duly warned and held for that purpose.

Approved, July 1st, 1873.

AN ACT IN RELATION TO APPEALS AND ASSESSMENTS MADE BY THE BOARD OF STREET COMMISSIONERS OF THE CITIES OF HARTFORD AND NEW BRITAIN.

Be it enacted by the Senate and House of Representatives in General Assembly convened :

All appeals now taken, or which may hereafter be taken from any appraisal of damages, or assessment of benefits made by the board of street commissioners of the city of Hartford, and the city of New Britain, to the judge of the court of common pleas for the county of Hartford, and which shall be pending at the time of the completion of the term of service of such judge, shall be heard and disposed of as fully and completely by the successor of such judge as said appeals might have been by the judge to whom they were originally taken.

Approved, June 18th, 1875.

ORDINANCES,

AND

STANDING RULES OF THE COMMON COUNCIL.

10

ORDINANCES.

CHAPTER I.

ACCOUNTS AND CLAIMS.

Be it ordained by the Common Council of the City of New Britain:

SECTION 1. No account shall be contracted in behalf of said city, or, if contracted, shall be of any binding force, unless the person so contracting be duly authorized by the charter of the city, or some order or ordinance of the Common Council, or by the committee of supplies thereof.

SEC. 2. No bills presented against said city shall be approved, or paid, unless the same shall have been legally contracted, nor unless they shall, so far as may be, contain detailed items and dates.

SEC. 3. No order shall be drawn by the Auditor upon the Treasurer without a previous vote of the Common Council authorizing the same, and the only evidence of such authority shall be a certified copy of such vote, which it shall be the duty of the City Clerk to deliver forthwith to the Auditor. All orders so drawn shall specify the nature of the claims for which they are respectively drawn.

SEC. 4. No money shall be paid from the city treasury except upon the written order of the Auditor, specifying the nature of the claim, and any payment otherwise made shall not be binding upon said city : *provided*, however, that notes of said city, payable at bank, or interest on city notes, scrip, or certificates of debt, may be paid by the City Treasurer.

SEC. 5. The Treasurer shall pay all orders so drawn in the order in which they shall be presented. Whenever any money shall be paid into the treasury of said city, the Treasurer shall execute duplicate receipts therefor, one of which shall be delivered to the party paying said money, and the other deposited immediately with the City Clerk.

SEC. 6. All claims accruing against said city by reason of judicial proceedings, previously had, shall be certified by the City Attorney to be correct before being acted upon by the Common Council.

SEC. 7. All claims against said city for damages, in consequence of any public improvement, shall be certified by the City Clerk to be in accordance with the original award of damages on file in his office before being acted upon by the Common Council, and shall then be acted upon in the same manner as other bills against the city. In case any person, in whose favor such bill for damages is passed, shall refuse to accept the order drawn therefor, the Auditor shall forward such order to the Treasurer, who shall thereafter pay the same on demand of the person in whose favor it was drawn.

SEC. 8. It shall be the duty of the City Clerk to keep a record, in books provided specially for that purpose, of all accounts due said city from any and every source, excepting water rents, and fines, etc., at the police and city courts ; and to obtain from the Mayor, City Attorney, Street Commissioner, Chief of Police, and the chairmen of the various committees, and all other officers of said city, all necessary information, in relation to accounts due the city, that may come to their knowledge ; and it shall be the duty of the herein-named officers, on application, to give to the Clerk said necessary information.

SEC. 9. It shall be the duty of the City Clerk to render to the Common Council monthly statements, in detail, of all accounts due said city, except accounts due for city taxes, water rents, and fines. etc., connected with the city and police courts, and to put all bills due the city into the hands of the Chief of Police for collection.

SEC. 10. It shall be the duty of the Auditor to audit, annually, the accounts of every city officer, or other person, who receives funds on account of said city, except the accounts of the Treasurer.

SEC. 11.   The Mayor, Senior Alderman, and Treasurer of said city, and their successors, shall, *ex-officio*, be a committee, to be known as the Sinking Fund Committee, whose duty it shall be to receive, manage, and invest any funds that are now, or may hereafter be, appropriated to any sinking fund for the extinguishment of any indebtedness or liability of said city, and said committee shall report, annually, to the Council, at its first meeting in April, the condition of all such sinking funds, and the investment thereof, and such report shall be printed with the annual reports of the Mayor and the several departments.

SEC. 12.   The funds belonging to any sinking fund of said city shall not be used for any other purpose, except that for which said funds were particularly set apart and appropriated.

CHAPTER II.

AMUSEMENTS.

Be it ordained by the Common Council of the City of New Britain:

SECTION 1.   Every person who shall, without obtaining a license from the Common Council, or the committee appointed by them for that purpose, make, or knowingly aid, or assist in making, a public display of any sport, amusement, performance, concert, opera, or other public exhibition, within the limits of said city, shall forfeit and pay a penalty of not less than five nor more than one hundred dollars for each offense, and each separate exhibition shall be deemed a separate offense within the meaning of this ordinance.

SEC. 2.   Any person who shall keep and use, or suffer to be kept and used, for hire, in any premises occupied by him or under his control, in said city, any billiard table, or bowling alley, without a proper license in force therefor, shall forfeit and pay a penalty of five dollars for each offense, and a like penalty for every day during which such table or alley is so used.

SEC. 3. The committee on licenses of the Common Council shall have power, unless otherwise directed by said Council, to grant written licenses, to be issued as provided in section seven of this ordinance, to persons applying for the same, for keeping for hire billiard tables or bowling alleys, and for the exhibition of any such sport, public amusement, concert, opera, or other performance, as they, the said committee, shall consider proper to be licensed, and for such time as they shall deem fit, which license may, at any time, be revoked by the said committee, or by the Common Council.

SEC. 4. Such person, applying as aforesaid, shall pay to the clerk of said committee, for the use of said city, such license fee as the said committee shall deem proper to fix, and said decision shall be subject to revision by the Common Council, which may lessen or increase the same.

SEC. 5. No corporation or person, being the owner, proprietor, agent, or janitor of any public hall in said city, shall permit such hall to be used for the purpose of giving any concert, opera, play, or other public amusement or exhibition, without having first received, from the proprietor or agent of such concert, opera, play, or other amusement or exhibition, as aforesaid, a license, in writing, from the committee on licenses, and any person who shall, by so doing, offend against this ordinance, shall forfeit and pay a penalty of twenty-five dollars for each offense.

SEC. 6. Every place in said city wherein any public amusement, concert, opera, play, or other public exhibition shall be held, shall be deemed a public hall, within the meaning of this ordinance.

SEC. 7. The City Clerk shall be clerk of said committee on licenses, and, under their direction, shall issue all licenses granted by said committee, and shall pay over all moneys received therefor to the City Treasurer, as often as once a month, and shall keep a record of all licenses so issued, together with the date thereof, the name of the licensee, to whom given, the amount of money received therefor, and the name or style of the exhibition licensed, which date, price, and name of license and exhibition shall also appear on the face of the license, and it shall be the duty of the owner, proprietor, agent, or janitor receiving any such license, to return the same to the clerk of said committee as often as once in three months, to be by him examined and lodged on file, together with such record, in the office of the City Clerk ; but said clerk shall not be entitled to receive from the city any extra compensation for services rendered to said committee.

SEC. 8.   It shall be the duty of the said committee to adopt, for their guidance, a tariff of license fees adapted to the different grades and classes of exhibitions, from which they shall deviate only under circumstances appealing to their sound discretion.

SEC. 9.   All violations of this ordinance shall be forthwith reported to the City Attorney for prosecution.

CHAPTER III.

BILLS, PLACARDS, AND NOTICES.

Be it ordained by the Common Council of the City of New Britain :

SECTION 1.   No person shall post up, or in any manner affix, any bill, placard, or notice, either written or printed, upon any fence, bridge, wall, or post, or private bulletin-board, or upon any building in said city, without the previous consent of the occupant or owner thereof ; nor upon any building, sidewalk, curbstone, tree, fence, or post belonging to said city, without the consent of the Common Council ; and any person offending against any provision of this section, shall forfeit and pay a penalty of not less than five nor more than fifteen dollars for each offense.

SEC. 2.   It shall be lawful for the license committee of the Common Council, for a reasonable fee, to authorize any person, pursuing the calling of a bill-poster, to erect in the streets of said city, at such points and in such manner as the nuisance committee shall approve, boards or posts upon which to post bills and notices, in the exercise of his calling.

Sec. 3. Any person, who shall tear down, remove, or deface any written or printed bill, placard, or notice, posted up in conformity with this ordinance, shall forfeit and pay a penalty of not less than one nor more than ten dollars for each offense.

CHAPTER IV.

CONTRACTS.

Be it ordained by the Common Council of the City of New Britain:

Section 1. Whenever the Street Commissioner, or the Water Commissioners, or any other officer of said city, having charge of any public improvements, shall judge it to be for the interest of the city, such commissioner, commissioners, or other officer in charge, may make contracts for labor and materials for such public improvements, and such contracts, when ratified by the Common Council, shall be valid and binding on said city, and all contracts for such labor and materials shall be in writing and executed in triplicate, of which one shall be kept by the commissioner, commissioners, or other officer aforesaid, one delivered to the City Clerk, and kept on file, and one retained by the contractor: and no such commissioner, commissioners, or other officer having charge of any public improvements, shall have any interest, direct or indirect, in any contract relating thereto: nor shall such contract be executed, unless good and satisfactory security for the faithful performance of the same shall be given by the contractor, and approved by said commissioner, commissioners, or other officer in charge.

Sec. 2. The said commissioner, commissioners, or other officer in charge as aforesaid, when not otherwise specially authorized by the Common Council, shall advertise in one or more newspapers in said city, for sealed proposals for all such contracts, specifying the time and place, when and where the same shall be received : and such proposals, in order to be received and acted upon, shall set forth a specified sum or price to be paid for all such labor and materials, without condition, limitation, or alteration, and shall be accompanied with a bond with satisfactory sureties, payable to the Mayor and his successors in office, conditioned for the faithful execution of the proposal, if the same shall be accepted in behalf of the city.

SEC. 3. No such contract shall be assigned or transferred, without the written assent of the Mayor, and the officer or officers having charge of the public improvement to which such contract relates.

CHAPTER V.

DOGS.

Be it ordained by the Common Council of the City of New Britain :

SECTION 1. Any dog found at large at any time within the limits of said city, without a collar having the owner's name distinctly marked thereon, shall be killed.

SEC. 2. Any dog found at large within the limits of said city, between the first day of July and the first day of October, in any year, not securely muzzled, shall be killed.

SEC. 3. The owner or keeper of any dog, who shall allow the same to go at large in violation of this ordinance, shall forfeit and pay a penalty of not more than twenty dollars for each offense.

SEC. 4. It shall be lawful for any person, and shall be the duty of every policeman of said city, to kill any dog found at large in violation of the provisions of this ordinance.

CHAPTER VI.

FIRE.

Be it ordained by the Common Council of the City of New Britain :

SECTION 1.   The Fire Department of said city shall consist of a Chief Engineer and one Assistant Engineer, one fire police company, and such number of engine, hose, and hook and ladder companies, as the Common Council shall deem necessary to organize and establish.

SEC. 2.   The Chief Engineer and Assistant Engineer shall be chosen, annually, in the month of May, by the Common Council, and shall hold their offices until others are appointed in their stead, and the Chief Engineer shall be required to give bonds with sureties, in the sum of one thousand dollars, for the faithful performance of his duty as prescribed in this ordinance.

SEC. 3.   The Chief Engineer shall have the superintendence, care and direction of the fire engines, hose carts, hook and ladder trucks, hose, and all other fire apparatus belonging to said city; shall see that the same, with the houses in which they are stored, and the fire hydrants belonging to the city are kept in good order and repair, and ready for immediate use; shall procure all such instruments for extinguishing fires, and such other necessary supplies as the Common Council, through the committee on Fire Department, shall from time to time direct; shall see that all such instruments and supplies, including hydrants, hose, hose-couplings, wrenches, and all fittings and connections, are of proper size, kind, and quality, and adapted to each other, and in conformity with the standard adopted by the Common Council; shall have the sole command at fires over the Assistant Engineer, and all other members of the Fire Department, and all other persons present at fires, and shall direct all proper measures for the extinguishment of fires, protection of property, preservation of order, and the observance of all laws, ordinances, and regulations respecting fires, and whenever at any fire it shall be deemed necessary by the Chief Engineer to pull down or demolish any building, in order to prevent the spreading of fire, he shall order the same to be done, having first obtained the consent of the Mayor, or in his absence that of the senior Alderman. He shall also keep, or cause to be kept, fair and exact rolls of the respective companies, specifying the name, age, occupation, and residence, and the date of enlistment and discharge of each member of said department ; shall keep an account of all fires occurring in said city, and shall report, annually, to the Common Council at its first meeting in April, all fires that have occurred during the previous year, and the cause, or supposed cause of such fires, and the estimated damage in each; and such report shall be accompanied with a full inventory of all property belonging to said department, and with such recommendations as he shall deem important, and he shall perform such other duties connected with said department as the Common Council may from time to time require.

SEC. 4.   It shall be the duty of the Assistant Engineer to assist the Chief Engineer in the discharge of his duties, to receive and communicate his orders at a fire, and see that they are executed, and in the absence of the Chief Engineer, his duties and powers in case of fire shall devolve upon the Assistant Engineer, with the assistance of the foreman of the senior hose company present at such fire.

SEC. 5.   It shall be the duty of the Chief Engineer and Assistant Engineer to visit the different manufacturing establishments located in said city, as often as twice a year, and ascertain the location of all gates, hydrants, water pipes, hose and connections on said premises, and make record thereof if deemed necessary; to acquaint themselves with all means in use by said manufacturing establishments for the prevention or extinguishment of fires, and to make such suggestions to the proprietors as they may deem necessary, to more effectually provide means of access to, or escape from any building in case of fire, so as to prevent loss of life, and more effectually protect the property therein.

SEC. 6. The Chief Engineer and Assistant Engineer shall severally have all power and authority necessary to preserve order and enforce their commands at a fire, and may use such force and command, and require the aid and assistance of such person or persons as may be necessary for that purpose.

SEC. 7. The several fire companies shall consist of the following number of men, viz: fire police company, 12 men ; hose companies, 12 men each ; hook and ladder companies, 20 men each ; and one engineer, one fireman, and one driver for each steam fire engine. All members of said companies shall reside within the city limits, and shall be appointed by the Common Council upon the recommendation of the Chief Engineer and committee on Fire Department, but no person under the age of twenty-one years shall be a member of any of said companies, nor shall any enlistment be allowed for a less term than six months.

SEC. 8. The fire police company, and each hose and hook and ladder company, shall have a foreman, one assistant foreman, and a clerk, who shall be appointed from their own number by the Common Council, upon the recommendation of the Chief Engineer, and receive certificates of their appointment, signed by the Mayor, and hold their offices for one year, or until they are removed and others are appointed in their stead.

SEC. 9. Foremen of companies shall see that the apparatus committed to their care, the buildings in which the same are housed, and all articles in or belonging to the same, are kept neat and clean ; shall preserve order and discipline at all times in their respective companies, and enforce strict compliance with the by-laws of the company and the regulations of the department.

SEC. 10. The clerk of each company shall keep in a book, to be provided by the Common Council, a true and exact roll of the officers and members of such company, specifying the name, age, occupation, and residence, and date of the enlistment and discharge of each member; shall keep a faithful record of the delinquencies and fines of members, and furnish copies of the same to the Chief Engineer on the first days of January and July in each year, which being found and certified by him to be correct, shall be returned to the City Clerk, to be kept on file ; and all company books and papers, in the possession of any clerk, shall be deemed the property of the city, and shall be by him surrendered to the Chief Engineer, when so ordered by the Common Council ; and any clerk refusing to deliver said books and papers, when so ordered, shall forfeit and pay a penalty of twenty dollars.

SEC. 11. The seniority of each company in the Fire Department shall be as follows, to wit : Hose Company No. 1, Hose Company No. 2, Hook and Ladder Company, Hose Company No. 3—the several officers in said companies taking rank, and assuming command as provided in this ordinance.

SEC. 12. There shall be paid to the several members of the Fire Department, who shall faithfully perform their respective duties, the following compensation, to wit : To the Chief Engineer, at the rate of three hundred dollars per annum ; to the Assistant Engineer, at the rate of one hundred dollars per annum; to the engineer of each steam fire engine, at the rate of two hundred and fifty dollars per annum ; and to the fireman of the same, at the rate of one hundred dollars per annum ; and, except as otherwise provided in this ordinance, to the foreman of each company, at the rate of sixty dollars per annum, to each assistant foreman at the rate of fifty dollars per annum, and to every other member of a company at the rate of forty dollars per annum. But no person shall be entitled to any portion of the compensation hereby provided, until he has served in said department for six months at least, nor until the time appointed for the payment of the same, in the fourteenth section of this ordinance; and if, at the time such compensation becomes payable, any member of said department shall have incurred any penalty, fine, or forfeiture, for the violation of any provision of this ordinance, and shall not have paid the same, he shall be entitled to receive only so much of said compensation as shall remain after deducting the amount of such penalty, fine, or forfeiture.

SEC. 13. The officers and members of the fire police company, and of special hose companies Nos. 5, 6, and 7, when performing duty at a fire, shall be paid at the rate of twenty-five cents per hour, and the members of said companies, when on duty as aforesaid, and while going to and returning from any fire, shall be governed by and subject to this ordinance, in the same manner, and to the same extent, as the other members of the Fire Department.

Sec. 14. Payment of the compensation of members of the Fire Department shall be made in semi-annual installments, in the months of January and July; and, in order to facilitate the same, it shall be the duty of the City Clerk, on or before the 10th days of January and July, in each year, to make out a pay-roll, on which shall be entered the names of the Chief Engineer, Assistant Engineer, engineers and firemen of steam fire engines, and all officers and members of each company in said department, the date of appointment or enlistment, the number of months' service, and the amount due each, after deducting all penalties, fines, or forfeitures, if any, unpaid on said dates—said pay-roll to be made out from the reports of the clerks of the several companies, certified to by the Chief Engineer, which reports shall be kept on file. And when such pay-roll shall have been audited by the committee on claims, and payment ordered by the Common Council, an order shall be drawn by the Auditor on the Treasurer for the full amount of the same. And the Auditor shall pay said members of the Fire Department on a fixed day in the months of January and July, but shall not pay any moneys except upon signing of receipts on said pay-roll.

Sec. 15. The several companies shall be called out by their respective foremen for the exercise and inspection of their apparatus, and instruments belonging thereto, at such times and places as the Chief Engineer shall appoint, and, when so called out, shall be under the direction of the Chief Engineer, or, in his absence, of the Assistant Engineer; and if any fireman shall neglect to appear at the time and place so appointed, without an excuse satisfactory to the Chief Engineer, he shall forfeit and pay a fine of one dollar.

Sec. 16. Whenever a fire shall break out in said city, it shall be the duty of the officers and members of the several companies to repair forthwith to their respective engines, hose, hook and ladder carriages, and other apparatus, and convey them, in as orderly a manner as may be, to the fire; and, on their arrival at the fire, the officer in command shall report to the engineer in command as ready for duty—and on all such occasions they shall exert themselves in the most orderly manner possible, in working and managing said engines, hose, hooks and ladders, and other fire apparatus, and shall obey all orders of the Chief Engineer, or other officer in command, in relation thereto; and when their services at such fire shall be no longer required, shall return the apparatus to their respective places of deposit, and no apparatus, controlled by said city, shall be taken beyond the city limits, on the occasion of a fire, except by permission of the Chief or Assistant Engineer. Any officer or member of a company, who shall fail to be present at any fire, without an excuse satisfactory to the Chief Engineer, shall forfeit and pay a fine of one dollar for each offense, and any officer or member of a company, wilfully neglecting or refusing to perform any of the duties prescribed in this section, shall be liable to dismission from the Fire Department.

SEC. 17. It shall be the duty of the fire police to guard the approaches to any building or buildings on fire, with ropes or other apparatus, and, unless otherwise ordered by the Chief or Assistant Engineer, not to permit within the lines any person not a member of said department, the Mayor, the city police, and owners of the property excepted, and to perform such police and other duties as may be required of them by the Chief or Assistant Engineer ; and any person who shall force his way within such lines, against the orders of such police, shall be subject to instant arrest, and to such fine, not exceeding twenty dollars, as may be imposed by the police court ; and said fire police are hereby each empowered with the necessary authority to make such arrest.

SEC. 18. Any person who shall knowingly give a false alarm of fire in said city, or shall knowingly proclaim that any fire is extinguished, when it is not, shall forfeit and pay a penalty of not less than seven nor more than thirty dollars.

SEC. 19. The engines, carriages, and other apparatus of the Fire Department shall not be drawn upon the sidewalks, and, when such engines and carriages are returning to their houses, they shall take the right of the road, and racing, on such returns, shall not be allowed.

SEC. 20. It shall be the duty of the officers and members of the fire police company, and every other company, to see that the house occupied by them is not used as a place of resort or amusement, but only for the necessary business purposes of such company, in the performance of their duty as a branch of the Fire Department.

SEC. 21. No cards, dice, or other articles used for gaming, shall be brought into, or suffered to remain in any building used by any company in the Fire Department, nor shall any spirituous liquors be used therein, neither shall any such building be opened or occupied on Sunday, except in case of alarm of fire ; and the penalty for disregarding this section shall be the expulsion of the offending members from said department.

SEC. 22. Boys, and other persons, not members of the Fire Department, shall not be allowed to frequent the house of, nor run with, any company belonging to said department.

SEC. 23. Every person who shall have served, according to law, in the Fire Department, for six successive years, shall be entitled to receive a certificate thereof, signed by the Mayor and City Clerk, and any person receiving such certificate shall be considered an honorary member of the department, and entitled to wear such badge as may be designated by the Common Council.

SEC. 24. Each fire policeman and each fireman shall, within two weeks after recording his name, deposit the sum of one dollar with the Chief Engineer, who shall, upon receiving the same, issue a badge of membership, and the money so received shall be deposited by said Chief Engineer with the Treasurer of said city.

SEC. 25. Members of the Fire Department, when on duty at fires, shall wear their badges on the left breast, and without such badges will not be recognized as members of said department.

SEC. 26. Any member leaving the Fire Department and returning his badge in good condition to the Chief Engineer, shall receive from him an order on the Treasurer of said city, for the amount of his deposit, and any member failing to produce his badge upon leaving said department shall forfeit the amount so deposited.

SEC. 27. Any member losing his badge shall advertise the loss of the same in one or more newspapers, stating when and where lost with full description of the same.

SEC. 28. The Chief Engineer, with the consent of the committee on Fire Department, may grant permission to any company to take their apparatus beyond the limits of said city on an excursion, to be absent such length of time as they may direct, the safe return of the same to be guaranteed, either by effecting insurance thereon, or in such other manner as shall be satisfactory to said committee.

SEC. 29. Any person or persons who shall take or remove any of the ladders, or other implements for extinguishing fires, belonging to said city, from the places where deposited, except in case of fire, or shall use any such ladder or other implements, or cause the same to be used when so taken, shall forfeit and pay a penalty of five dollars.

SEC. 30.   The Chief Engineer, or in his absence the Assistant Engineer, with the approbation of the committee on the Fire Department, may, and for the second offense shall, dismiss from the said department any officer or member of any company for neglect of duty, drunkenness, disorderly conduct, disobedience of orders, or willful violation of any of the provisions of this ordinance, and such dismissed member shall not be entitled to compensation for his services.

SEC. 31.   There shall be, annually, in the month of May an inspection and parade of the Fire Department, at such time and place as the Mayor may direct.

SEC. 32.   Whenever it shall appear to the committee on the Fire Department, from report of the Chief Engineer or otherwise, that any building occupied in whole or in part for public use, or for a public hall, or for any other purpose, is unsafe by reason of insufficient facilities for egress in case of fire or other accident, or in consequence of the materials or mode of its construction, said committee shall notify the owners or occupiers thereof to provide for the same such scuttles, fire escapes, fire ladders, or other means of egress, or to make such alterations in said building, as in their opinion the reasonable safety of persons or property requires; such notice to be in writing and to specify the thing to be done, and a reasonable time not less than one month, within which the order must be complied with, and to be served by causing a copy thereof to be left at the usual place of abode of said owner or occupant, and a duplicate thereof to be lodged with the City Clerk. And every person who shall refuse or neglect to comply with such order within the time specified, shall forfeit and pay a penalty of ten dollars, and an additional penalty of ten dollars for every week during which such neglect or refusal shall continue: *provided*, however, that any person aggrieved by said order may appeal to the Common Council within the time limited in said order, and said Common Council may in their discretion affirm, modify, or rescind the same.

SEC. 33.   No person shall carry into or use in any barn, stable, or other building in said city, in which hay, straw, stalks, husks, or other combustible material is deposited or kept, any lighted candle, lamp, or fire, unless the same shall be well secured in a lantern, nor carry into or use in such building any lighted pipe

12

or cigar, nor throw down or drop therein any matches unused or with any fire on them, nor keep therein any matches except in a fire-proof box or match safe, nor throw or drop therein any fire-crackers, or fire-works of any kind. And every person who shall violate any of the foregoing provisions of this section shall forfeit and pay a penalty of not less than five nor more than one hundred dollars for each offense.

· Sec. 34. Every person who shall use or explode any fire-crackers or fire-works of any kind, or make, or assist in making or kindling, any bonfire in any street or public park of said city, without the written consent of the Chief of Police countersigned by the Mayor, shall forfeit and pay a penalty of five dollars for each offense.

Sec. 35. No person shall discharge any gun, pistol, cannon, or other fire-arms of any sort or description within the limits of said city unless by written permission of the Chief of Police, or by order of some military officer on occasion of military exercises and parade, and such permit of said Chief of Police shall state the date, length of time of such permit, and the name of the person, club, or organization to whom such permission is granted, and a record thereof shall be kept by the Chief of Police in a book provided for the purpose, and whoever shall discharge any pistol, gun or cannon, or other fire-arm, without permission as aforesaid, shall for each offense forfeit and pay a penalty of five dollars.

Sec. 36. Any person who shall discharge any fire-works so as to annoy and cause serious discomfort to any inhabitant of said city, shall forfeit and pay for each offense, a penalty of five dollars.

Sec. 37. If any minor or apprentice shall be guilty of a breach of any of the provisions of this ordinance, the parent, guardian, or master of such minor or apprentice, shall be liable to pay the forfeiture incurred thereby, and may be sued therefor in a proper action brought in the name of said city upon this ordinance.

Sec. 38. If any person, persons, or corporations, shall, without permission of the Common Council, erect, add to, move or station any building excepting privies, of which either outer wall, or the outer covering of the roof is composed of wood or any other combustible material, within the area included within the following named streets and lines, and where said streets and lines do not coincide with the limits of said city, extending in the direction of said city limits two hundred feet beyond said streets and lines, to wit : beginning at the junction of Park and South Stanley streets, thence along South Stanley street to Whiting street, thence along Whiting street to South Main street, thence along South Main street to Ellis street, thence along Ellis street to Glen street, thence along Glen street to Locust street, thence along Locust street to Kensington street, thence across Kensington street into Arch street, thence along Arch street to Winthrop street, thence along Winthrop street to Linwood street, thence along Linwood street to Hart street, thence along Hart street to Vine street, thence along Vine street to West Main street, thence along West Main street to Curtis street, thence along Curtis street to Broad street, thence along Broad street to Beaver street, thence northerly along Beaver street to the city limits, thence along the line of said city limits to Lawlor street, thence along Lawlor street to North street, thence along North street to Elm street, thence across Elm street to North Stanley street, thence along North Stanley street to the aforesaid Park street, the place of beginning—such person, persons, or corporations shall forfeit and pay a penalty of fifty dollars, and a further penalty of fifty dollars for each period of ten days, during which such building or addition to a building shall be continued without such permission, and the continuance of any such building or part of building for each period of ten days as aforesaid, shall be deemed a separate and distinct offense.

CHAPTER VII.

GOOD ORDER AND DECENCY.

SECTION	SECTION
1. Billiard-rooms, bowling-alleys, saloons, &c., when to be closed.	2. Violation of ordinance and of statute relating to the Sabbath, by whom reported and prosecuted.

Be it ordained by the Common Council of the City of New Britain:

SECTION 1. All bar-rooms, billiard-rooms, bowling-saloons, and all places where spirituous or intoxicating liquors are commonly kept and sold in said city, shall be closed at the hour of ten and one-half o'clock in the evening of each day, and shall be kept closed until five o'clock in the morning of the next day; and any proprietor or occupant of any such bar-room, or billiard-saloon, or bowling-saloon, or place where spirituous or intoxicating liquors are commonly kept and sold, who shall neglect or refuse to close the same at the hour for closing aforesaid, and keep the same closed during the whole before-mentioned period, shall forfeit and pay for each offense a penalty not exceeding twenty-five dollars.

SEC. 2.   It shall be the duty of the Chief of Police and all other police officers of said city, to report to the City Attorney all violations of this ordinance, and also all violations of the 60th Section of Chapter IX, Title XX, of the Revised Statutes of the State of Connecticut, revision of 1875, being an act for the due observance of the Sabbath or Lord's day, and the City Attorney is hereby directed to prosecute the same.

CHAPTER VIII.

HEALTH.

SECTION 1.   Health Committee, appointment and duties.

Be it ordained by the Common Council of the City of New Britain:

SECTION 1.   The Common Council shall annually appoint not exceeding five persons, who may or may not be members thereof, to be denominated the Health Committee, whose duty it shall be to cause all nuisances injurious to the public health, to be removed or suppressed, and said committee and any two of them, are hereby empowered to inspect, as often as they deem necessary, all markets, shops, and other places in said city, and whenever they shall find filth or putrefaction in any market, shop, or other place by them visited, which in their opinion may prove detrimental to the health of the inhabitants of said city or any portion thereof, said committee, or any two of them, shall give orders to the persons owning or occupying said market, shop, or place in which said filth or putrefaction shall be found, to remove or bury the same, or to cleanse or purify such market, shop, or other place, in such other way or manner as said committee, or said two of them there present, may deem advisable ; and said committee, or said two of them, are hereby empowered to give orders to the person or persons owning or occupying such markets, shops, or other places, in relation to the ways and means to be by them used, in order to keep the same continually cleansed and purified from filth and putrefaction; and all orders and directions given by said committee, or said two of them, as aforesaid, shall be in writing, and a duplicate thereof be lodged with the City Clerk by said committee, immediately after the delivery of such orders and directions to the person or persons aforesaid ; and every person who shall neglect to obey and conform to any of said orders and directions, or any part thereof, so given in conformity to this ordinance, shall forfeit and pay a penalty not exceeding ten dollars for every day that such person shall so neglect and refuse to comply ; and said committee shall report every violation of this ordinance to the City Attorney, and it shall be the duty of said Attorney to prosecute the same.

CHAPTER IX.

JURORS OF THE CITY COURT.

SECTION 1. Penalty for neglecting to serve when summoned.

Be it ordained by the Common Council of the City of New Britain :

SECTION 1. Every juror of said city, who, being legally summoned and returned to serve as a juryman at any city court in said city, shall refuse or neglect to attend and perform such service agreeably to such summons, shall forfeit and pay a penalty of five dollars to the City Treasurer, unless the court shall, on hearing his reasons for non-attendance, judge the same to be sufficient.

CHAPTER X.

MEETINGS OF THE CITY AND COMMON COUNCIL.

Be it ordained by the Common Council of the City of New Britain:

SECTION 1.   There shall be stated monthly meetings of the Common Council, at the Common Council room in said city, for the transaction of all legal business, on the third Wednesday evening of each month, and a stated annual meeting for the choice of jurors, on the third Wednesday in June.

SEC. 2.   The Mayor, or in case of his absence or disability, the senior Alderman present in said city may at any time, and when thereunto instructed by the Common Council, shall call a city meeting ; and may at any time, and upon the request in writing of any two Aldermen and four Councilmen, shall, without delay, call a meeting of the Common Council, which meeting shall be called by issuing a warrant to the sheriff, or any suitable person named therein, requiring him to notify the electors of said city, or the members of the Common Council, as the case may be, that such meeting will be held at the time and place in such warrant designated.   All warrants, in the case of city meetings, shall specify the object thereof, and shall be served at least three days before the day when such meeting is to be held, by causing a true and attested copy thereof to be published in at least one newspaper published in said city, and by posting a like copy upon the public sign-post therein ; and shall be forthwith returned with proper indorsement, to the City Clerk, and be by him recorded : and all warrants for meetings of the Common Council, shall be served by reading the same in the hearing of each member, or by leaving a copy thereof at his usual place of abode ; and shall be forthwith returned with a proper indorsement, to the City Clerk, and be by him recorded.

SEC. 3.   All stated meetings of the Common Council, and all special meetings thereof, when not otherwise provided in the warning, shall commence at seven o'clock in the evening, if held between noon of the first day of November and noon of the first day of March thereafter, and at seven and one-half o'clock in the evening, if held at any.other time in the year.

SEC. 4.   The City Clerk shall make and keep true records, properly indexed, of all proceedings of said City and Common Council.

CHAPTER XI.

NUISANCE.

Be it ordained by the Common Council of the City of New Britain:

SECTION 1. The following acts, when committed within said city, are declared to be acts of nuisance, to wit : keeping swine in any pen, sty, or other place in such manner that the same shall become unwholesome or offensive to any person; causing or permitting the accumulation, in any building, outhouse, yard, or enclosure, of any dung, filth, manure, offal, wash, dirty water, or brine, which shall become offensive to any person; setting up or continuing any privy in such place or manner that the same shall become unwholesome or offensive to any person; causing or permitting wash or dirty water to pass from yards or houses, through drains or otherwise, into any street, or upon any sidewalk of said city; depositing any offal, dead animal, animal matter, decayed or decaying vegetable matter, or garbage, in any street, public park, stream, or pond in said city. or conveying through any street thereof any offal, or dead animal, unless covered from sight; fastening any animal to any tree, or leaving any animal so that any tree in said city shall be injured by such animal; erecting, setting up, or continuing upon any street or highway, or any portion of the same, any building, fence, or gate; causing or permitting any wagon, cart, or other vehicle, or any animal to remain stationary upon any crosswalk in said city, or riding, driving, or leading any horse or other animal upon any sidewalk thereof; riding or driving any horse or horses, in harness or otherwise, upon, over, or across any sidewalk at a gait faster than a walk; injuring, defacing, or soiling any public or private building, fence, or enclosure; injuring any tree, shrub, plant, or other vegetable production in the streets or in public or private enclosures in said city; making any loud or boisterous noise in the night season in any street, building, or other place, whereby any person is disturbed; ringing hand-bells in any street of said city, to advertise auction or other sales; trespassing in any garden or yard in said city; placing any mortar-bed, or placing or continuing the deposit of any building material in any street in said city without license from the Common Council; racing or trying the speed of horses upon any street in said city; carrying on of any trade or business upon the sidewalks, or streets, without license therefor; resisting, molesting, or disturbing any executive or police officer or Street Commissioner of said city while discharging his duty; placing any sign across any sidewalk without permission from the Common Council; assembling idly and remaining in crowds upon any footway, sidewalk, or crosswalk in any street, or in any public park of said city, or before any church or public building; so assembling to the number of three or more persons, and refusing to disperse when commanded so to do by a police officer, special constable, or other officer of said city; sliding down hill upon sleds or otherwise, upon any of the following streets, to wit: Main street, West Main street, Beaver street, Sexton street, Clark street, Lawlor street, North street, Broad street, Walnut street, Grand street, School street, Hart street, or any other street in which there is any passenger or vehicle at the time; throwing or playing with any ball upon any public street; discharging the contents of any privy, water-closet, sink-drain or sewer into the bed of the stream appropriated by said city, between the foundry of the Russell & Erwin Manufacturing Company at the commencement of the main sewer and the junction of said stream with the lower ditch near the land of John Hanna, and between East Main and North street; accumulating in or near any building, shavings, hay, husks, straw, or other combustible materials in such a manner as to endanger property from fire; depositing or keeping hay, straw, husks, or other combustible materials in any building occupied wholly or in part as a dwelling.

And any person doing or committing any of said acts, or who shall knowingly aid or assist in the commission of the same, shall forfeit and pay a penalty of not more than twenty nor less than three dollars for each offense, and each day's continuance of any continuing nuisance, herein before mentioned, shall constitute a separate and distinct offense.

SEC. 2. Any animal that shall die or be found dead in said city, except when such animal has been killed for food, shall be properly buried by the owner thereof upon notice by the police, and when such owner is not known, or, being notified as aforesaid, shall neglect or refuse to bury said animal, the same shall be buried by the police at the expense of the city; and any person so neglecting or refusing shall forfeit and pay a penalty of not less than five nor more than twenty dollars.

Sec. 3. No person, without the consent of the Health Committee, shall convey the contents of any privy-vault, or cess-pool, through any street of said city, except in a tight box, and between the first day of November and the first day of April then next succeeding, and between the hours of nine and five o'clock, in the night season; and any person so offending shall forfeit and pay a penalty of five dollars for each offense.

Sec. 4. No person, without the consent of the Health Committee, shall build, or maintain any privy or cess-pool in said city, within twenty-five feet of any street line or dwelling house, or public building, nor without leaving at least two feet of solid earth or mason work, laid in cement, between such privy or cesspool and the lot adjoining.

Sec. 5. No privy shall hereafter be· erected or suffered to remain in said city, unless connected with some public sewer, or unless kept clean by means of fresh earth or other disinfectant, or without having a vault under the same of the depth of at least six feet of the full length and width of such privy, and closed up on all sides; nor shall said vault be suffered to be at any time filled within three feet of the general surface of the ground around such privy; and any person offending against the provisions of this section, and of section fourth of this ordinance, shall forfeit and pay a penalty of not less than five nor more than twenty dollars for each offense, and each week's continuance thereof shall be deemed a separate offense.

CHAPTER XII.

ORDINANCES.

13

Be it ordained by the Common Council of the City of New Britain:

SECTION 1. Every ordinance of said city shall be twice published in a newspaper in said city.

SEC. 2. No ordinance shall be valid and operative until it has been once so published. •

SEC. 3. All orders and notices requiring publication by the city charter; and all orders and notices ordered published by the Common Council; and all orders and notices published by order of the Street Commissioner or any other city officer, in any newspaper, shall not be published more than twice in such paper, except by special order of the Common Council.

SEC. 4. The ordinances of said city, as nearly as practicable, shall be entitled and arranged alphabetically according to the subject-matter, and all new ordinances and amendments of ordinances shall be printed with the annual reports of the Mayor and several departments. •

SEC. 5. All the ordinances of said city in force on the 31st day of December, A. D. 1876, shall hereby be repealed; but no offense committed, and no liability, penalty, or forfeiture heretofore incurred, and no tax or assessment heretofore laid or incurred, and no prosecution or suit pending, shall be affected, and no ordinance heretofore repealed, shall be revived by this repeal.

CHAPTER XIII.

POLICE.

Be it ordained by the Common Council of the City of New Britain:

SECTION 1. There shall be, and hereby is established a police force for said city, which shall consist of a captain, to be called the Chief of Police, a Lieutenant of Police, and not more than eight active policemen, and not less than ten nor more than twenty supernumerary policemen.

SEC. 2.   It shall be the duty of the Chief of Police to superintend, under the direction of the Mayor, the entire police force; to inform himself of the fidelity and efficiency of every member thereof; to have charge of and be responsible for the condition of the station house and its furniture; to supply the same with lights and fuel, and the inmates, if any, with necessary food, at the expense of said city; to attend on the Police Court; to receive from members of said force all complaints of violations of the public law or the city ordinances, and see that the same are prosecuted; to report all cases requiring a written complaint to the City Attorney or his assistant, or in their absence, to a grand juror; to designate a supernumerary policeman to take the place of any active policeman absent from duty; to call into active service the supernumerary police, or any portion of the same, when authorized thereto by the acting Mayor; to keep a roll of the members of said force, and to report to the Common Council, annually, at its first meeting in April, and at other times when called upon, the exact condition thereof, together with the number and causes of arrest or detention since the last previous report; to be present at all fires in said city, and assist thereat in the preservation of order and the protection of life and property; and in all legal ways to guard the peace of said city.

SEC. 3.   In case of the absence from said city of the Chief of Police or his inability to discharge the duties required of him by this ordinance, the Lieutenant of Police shall, during such absence or inability, be acting Chief of Police.

SEC. 4.   It shall be the duty of policemen to obey all lawful orders and directions of the Mayor or Chief of Police; to engage in no private business; to guard the city day and night; to report to the Chief of Police all violations of the laws of the State, and ordinances of said city, all suspicious persons, all houses of ill-fame, all gaming houses, all disorderly and suspicious places of resort; to preserve the public peace; to secure the detection, arrest, and conviction of offenders, and render all possible assistance to the ministers of the law; to be present and on duty at all fires in said city, when not otherwise specially employed; to serve processes of the Police Court and notices ordered by the Common Council; to direct strangers the nearest way to their places of destination; to keep open and free from obstruction by vehicles, crowds, or groups of persons, or other things, the streets, sidewalks, and public places of said city; and in general to perform the duties assigned them in these ordinances, and do all in their power to preserve the peace and protect life and property.

SEC. 5. The Chief of Police and other members of the police force shall wear, when on duty, their distinguishing badges, as prescribed by the Common Council.

SEC. 6. No fee or compensation, other than the regular pay, shall be charged or received by any member of the police force, but each member shall, before entering upon the discharge of the duties of his office, execute in writing an assignment to the Treasurer of said city of all his interest in any fees which may be taxed in his favor in the Police or City Court in causes in which said city is a party, and no member of the force shall be entitled to receive any salary for any services rendered by him, until such assignment shall have been executed to the satisfaction of the Committee on Police of the Common Council, and lodged on file in the office of the City Clerk; nor shall any member of the force receive any present or reward for services rendered, or to be rendered, by him unless with the consent of the Common Council.

SEC. 7. Every member of the police force shall, at the time of his appointment, be a citizen of the United States and able to speak, read, and write the English language, and shall, before entering upon the discharge of the duties of his office, make oath or affirmation, before some competent authority, that he will support the Constitution of the United States, and of the State of Connecticut, and will faithfully discharge the duties of his office, and shall cause a certificate of such oath or affirmation to be lodged with the City Clerk.

SEC. 8. The pay of the Chief of Police shall be nine hundred dollars per year. The pay of the Lieutenant of Police and of each policeman shall be eight hundred dollars per year, and at the same rate for each supernumerary for each day of actual service.

SEC. 9. The willful breach of any law of this State, or ordinance of said city, neglect of duty, inefficiency, intoxication, insubordination, frequenting, drinking, or playing at games in saloons, or other places where liquors are exposed for sale, or any other disgraceful or improper conduct which will bring discredit on the police force or impair its usefulness, shall be considered sufficient cause for the preferment of charges against the officer so offending, under the provisions of the charter of said city.

SEC. 10. Any policeman who shall act as Constable of the town of New Britain, or who shall act as any other officer, of said town, in any capacity in which he is entitled to receive salary, fees, or emoluments, or who shall engage in any private business, shall be deemed to have tendered his resignation as policeman, and the same shall be accepted by the Common Council, and his place as policeman be filled or declared vacant.

CHAPTER XIV.

PUBLIC CONVEYANCES.

Be it ordained by the Common Council of the City of New Britain:

SECTION 1. Every hack, omnibus, cab, coach, barouche, or other vehicle on wheels or on runners and drawn by one or more animals, which shall be used in said city for carrying persons for hire, shall be deemed a public carriage within the meaning of this ordinance.

SEC. 2. No public carriage shall be used within the limits of said city, and no baggage wagon, express wagon, cart, dray or truck, or other vehicle on wheels or runners, shall be used or employed to convey for hire any baggage, goods, wares, merchandise, freights or materials from place to place in said city, unless the same shall be duly licensed by the Chief of Police, and every such license shall be in writing, and expire on the first Monday of May succeeding its date, and shall be recorded before being issued by said Chief of Police in a book kept for the purpose.

SEC. 3. No public carriage or other vehicle shall be licensed as aforesaid, until the owner thereof shall have paid the Treasurer of said city a license fee as follows: namely, for each public carriage or other vehicle drawn by two or more horses or other animals, two dollars, drawn by one animal, one dollar, and the receipt of the Treasurer for the same shall be filed with the Chief of Police, and shall be sufficient evidence of the payment of the aforesaid fee.

SEC. 4. The rates of fare to be charged by the proprietors or drivers of public carriages shall not exceed the following, to wit: for carrying each person with one trunk, a carpet-bag, a hat-box, or similar article, any distance within the limits of said city not exceeding one-half of one mile, twenty-five cents, for carrying a greater distance than half a mile, one passenger with baggage as aforesaid, fifty cents, and two passengers traveling together, each with baggage as aforesaid, seventy-five cents, and for each additional passenger belonging to the same party, twenty-five cents; for carrying children between the ages of four and twelve years one-half the above rates only shall be charged; for the use of a public carriage by the hour, two dollars, and at the same rate for fractions of an hour, after the first hour; for going to and from funerals, three dollars, and for attending upon weddings, two dollars.

SEC. 5. The name of the owner, the number of the license and the rates of fare, as prescribed by this ordinance, shall be conspicuously exhibited upon a card placed upon the inside of each public carriage, and the number of said license shall also be fastened or painted conspicuously upon the outside, and upon each side of said vehicle, and the number of the license, and the name of the owner, shall be fastened or painted conspicuously upon the outside of every other licensed vehicle.

SEC. 6. Every person, whether the owner or driver of a public carriage or other vehicle, who shall violate any of the provisions of this ordinance, shall forfeit and pay for each offense a penalty of not less than five nor more than twenty-five dollars.

CHAPTER XV.

SALARIES AND BONDS.

Be it ordained by the Common Council of the City of New Britain:

SECTION 1. The salaries of the several officers, and the fees for the several services hereinafter mentioned, shall be as follows, to wit: the City Clerk, eight hundred dollars per annum; the Judge of the City and Police Courts, eight hundred dollars per annum; the Auditor, one hundred dollars per annum; the Clerk of the Police Court, three hundred dollars per annum; the Collector of taxes, two per cent. on the amount of taxes collected; the City Attorney, a retainer of one hundred dollars and fees, as provided in section second.

SEC. 2. The following fees shall be paid:

To the City Sheriff,

For each day's attendance of City Court, $1.50.

For summoning a jury, same as other legal processes.

For warning a city meeting, $1.00.

For warning a meeting of the Common Council, $1.00.

For serving processes, the same as sheriffs.

To the City Attorney,

For complaint and attendance before the Police Court, the same fees allowed grand jurors for like services.

For each trial in the Police Court in which the accused shall appear by counsel, $3.00.

For other services, usual fees, to be approved by the Common Council.

SEC. 3. The City Auditor shall draw his order monthly on the City Treasurer for the payment of each member of the police force, and for the salaries of all other city officers: *provided*, that the bills presented to the Auditor by the said officers for their respective salaries shall each be separately approved by the Mayor.

SEC. 4. All bonds of city officers shall be payable in said city to the Mayor and his successors in office, and shall be executed by the principal, and when not otherwise provided, two sufficient sureties to the approbation of the Mayor and aldermen; such bond shall be conditioned on the faithful performance by the principal of all his official duties due to said city by virtue of his appointment, and on his saving the city harmless from all loss, cost, or damage, by reason of his malfeasance in office, and on his rendering a true account of all his money dealings for, in behalf of, and with said city, and on his just and true payment to the City Treasurer of all moneys in his hands at any time as an officer or agent of said city, for and during the entire period for which he shall remain in his office by appointment or election. Such bonds shall be given before such officer shall enter upon his official duties, and in case of the refusal or neglect of such officer to give such bonds, his office shall be deemed vacant.

SEC. 5. The penalties of the bonds required of the several city officers shall be respectively as follows: of the City Treasurer, five thousand dollars; of the City Collector, three thousand dollars; of the Clerk of the City and Police Courts, one thousand dollars, and of the City Sheriff, two thousand dollars.

SEC. 6. Every committee and every city officer, in whose hands money may be placed for disbursement, shall, unless otherwise provided in these ordinances, first give bonds to said city for the faithful disbursement of the same, in such sums as the Mayor and aldermen shall require.

CHAPTER XVI.

SEWERS.

Be it ordained by the Common Council of the City of New Britain :

SECTION 1. Each member of the Board of Sewer Commissioners shall receive three dollars for each day of actual employment in the duties of his office, and shall report monthly to the Common Council the number of days of said employment during the previous month.

SEC. 2. Each member of said Board of Sewer Commissioners shall give bond, with at least one sufficient surety, in the sum of three thousand dollars, for the faithful performance of his duty.

SEC. 3. Said Board of Sewer Commissioners shall keep a record of their official doings, and report the same annually to the Common Council, at its first meeting in April.

SEC. 4. No person or corporation shall make any connection of sewers or drains with any public sewers without written permission, signed by a majority of the members of the Board of Sewer Commissioners. And any person offending against the provisions of this section shall forfeit and pay a penalty of one hundred dollars for each offense.

CHAPTER XVII.

STREETS.

Be it ordained by the Common Council of the City of New Britain :

SECTION 1. Each member of the Board of Street Commissioners shall receive at the rate of three dollars for each day of actual employment in the duties of his office, and shall report monthly the number of days of said employment during the previous month.

SEC. 2. The Board of Street Commissioners shall appoint a Clerk, whose duty it shall be to keep a record of the doings of said Board in a book provided for that purpose, and the compensation of said Clerk shall be one hundred dollars per annum.

SEC. 3. Before making any assessment of damages and benefits, said Board of Street Commissioners shall give written notice to the parties interested of the time and place when and where they will meet to hear them, which notice shall be served by any proper officer or indifferent person by reading the same in the hearing of each party to be notified, or by leaving a copy thereof with him, or at his usual place of abode, at least three days before the date of such hearing.

SEC. 4. There shall be an officer appointed for said city, to be called the Street Commissioner, who shall be elected annually in the month of April, shall be sworn to a faithful discharge of his duty, and shall give bond, with sureties, in the sum of one thousand dollars.

SEC. 5. It shall be the duty of the Street Commissioner to execute, and supervise the execution of, all orders and directions of the Common Council relative to the construction, completion, altera-

14

tion or repair of all streets, highways, sidewalks, gutters, cross-walks, and sewers, in said city, when not otherwise expressly ordered to be done by other officers or persons; to keep all public places and thoroughfares free from nuisances, and from danger to persons and property, by causing the immediate repair of all de-fects and the prompt removal of all obstructions, encroachments, encumbrances, and filth therein, and by reporting for prosecution all violations of city ordinances relating thereto; to prescribe the terms and manner of excavating streets and highways, for laying down and taking up gas pipes, water pipes, and private sewers, and con-necting private sewers with public sewers, also the manner of moving buildings through the public streets and highways; to keep a record of complaints, and faithfully enter therein all complaints made to him concerning streets, sidewalks, and all public places, and the breach of ordinances and orders relating thereto; to con-form to all general rules and special directions of the Common Council relating to the locality, measurements, and materials of public work; to keep an accurate account of expenditures in his department, to be open at all times to the inspection of any mem-ber of the Common Council, to make a written report, annually, to the Common Council, at its first meeting in April, of labors and expenditures of the previous year, with an approximate estimate of the expenses of his department for the year ensuing; and to impart at any time any information in his power which the Council may call for concerning his official action, or the condition of his department; to employ all assistants that the discharge of his duties may require; and to make provisional contracts, subject to the approval of the Common Council, for such public works connected with highways, streets, crosswalks, sidewalks, gutters, and sewers, as ought in his judgment to be done by contract.

SEC. 6. It shall be the duty of the Street Commissioner to make out a pay-roll each month, on which shall be entered the name of every workman, the number of hours of work of each, and the place where such work was done, including teams, if any, price per hour, and amount. And when such pay-roll shall have been audited by the Committee on Claims, and payment ordered by the Common Council, an order shall be drawn by the Auditor for the full amount of the same, and the Auditor shall draw the money on said order, and shall pay workmen on a fixed day, each month, but shall not pay any moneys except upon the signing of a receipt by each workman, on said pay-roll, unless by special order of the Common Council.

SEC. 7. Every person who shall, without the consent of the Street Commissioner, or of the Common Council, dig up or excavate any portion of the streets, highways, sidewalks, or gutters of said city, or shall place thereon any earth, stones, rubbish, or other obstruction to the public use or travel, or shall aid, assist, or abet in any of said acts, shall for each offense pay a penalty of ten dollars.

SEC. 8. Every person who, after having been notified by the Street Commissioner to fill up any excavation or opening in any of the highways, streets, sidewalks, or gutters of said city, made, or procured to be made by him, or to remove therefrom any obstructions, rubbish, earth, or stones placed thereon by him, or by his procurement, shall neglect or refuse so to do within the time limited in such notice, shall pay for each offense a penalty of ten dollars; and such neglect or refusal for each twenty-four hours after the expiration of the time limited in such notice, shall be deemed a separate and distinct offense.

SEC. 9. The compensation of the Street Commissioner shall be three dollars per day for each day of actual service, and he shall report monthly to the Common Council the number of days of actual service during the preceding month.

SEC. 10. No street, or public thoroughfare, or part of any street, or public thoroughfare, shall be laid out or opened to the public use within the limits of said city, except by the direction of, or with the consent of, the Common Council first obtained, and if any person or corporation shall lay out or open any street, or public thoroughfare, or part of any street, or public thoroughfare within the limits of said city, without such consent or direction, such person or corporation so offending shall forfeit and pay a penalty of fifty dollars, and a further penalty of fifty dollars for each period of ten days during which such street, or part of street, public thoroughfare, or part of a public thoroughfare, shall remain open and accessible to the public, and the original opening aforesaid, and each continuance of ten days, as aforesaid, shall constitute a separate and distinct offense.

SEC. 11. Every person or corporation owning or occupying any land fronting upon any sidewalk within said city, shall, within six hours of daylight immediately following the cessation of any fall of snow or accumulation of ice thereon, cause the same to be removed, so that the passing upon said sidewalk shall not be obstructed, dangerous, or inconvenient; and upon failure so to do within the time limited, shall forfeit and pay a fine of five dollars ; and after the expiration of the time limited, as aforesaid, if such snow or ice shall not have been removed, it shall be the duty of the Street Commissioner to remove the same at the expense of such owner or occupier; and such expense shall be recoverable of the owner or occupier in default, as aforesaid, by an action brought upon this ordinance in the name of said city.

Sec. 12. Whenever any lumber, brick, mortar, or other materials used in building, shall necessarily be left out over night in any street of said city, whether with the consent of the Common Council or otherwise, the owner thereof shall cause to be placed over or near the same, in some conspicuous place, a large, well-lighted lamp or lantern. which shall be kept burning from dark to daybreak; and every person offending against this provision of this ordinance shall forfeit and pay a penalty of ten dollars for each offense.

Sec. 13. Any person who shall willfully or maliciously cut, break. injure, destroy, or deface any gas-light, lamp, lantern, post, or frame, erected or maintained by the Common Council for the purpose of lighting the streets of said city, or shall light or extinguish any public gas-lamp or other light without proper authority, or in any way willfully or maliciously interfere with the proper use or management of the public lights in said city, shall forfeit and pay a penalty of fifteen dollars for each offense.

CHAPTER XVIII.

TAXES.

Be it ordained by the Common Council of the City of New Britain:

Section 1. Whenever said city shall lay a tax, the same shall be levied upon the polls and ratable estate liable to taxation therein, as set and entered in the assessment list of the town of New Britain last made and completed.

SEC. 2. It shall be the duty of the finance committee of the Common Council, when any city tax shall be laid, to cause to be prepared by some proper person to be called the city rate-bill maker, a full and complete city assessment list, in preparing which list no change shall be made from the valuations in said town list: *provided*, however, that when it shall appear that any real estate, assessed in said town list as one parcel, is situated partly within and partly without said city, or that any real estate situated wholly within said city has been omitted from said town list, or that any real estate has changed ownership since said town list was made, then in either of said cases, the finance committee of the Common Council shall apply to one or more of the town assessors for the time being, who shall assess the value of such real estate, and the same shall be placed in the city assessment list at the valuation so established, and the value as so fixed of any transferred real estate shall be deducted from the list of the person in whose name it stood on said town assessment list. The said city list being so prepared, shall be deposited with the City Clerk and, within twenty days thereafter, the finance committee shall meet at some convenient place in said city, having given notice of the time and place of such meeting in a newspaper in said city, at least ten days before holding the same, to hear and act upon the complaints of all persons or corporations claiming to be aggrieved by such amendatory action of said assessors or their failure to amend said list on application as aforesaid, and for that purpose shall have the powers of town boards of relief; and said city assessment being so perfected by the finance committee and certified by them, shall be lodged with the City Clerk, and shall be the basis of taxation by said city until the next town assessment shall have been made and completed. It shall also be the duty of said rate-bill maker to make out and certify a rate-bill setting forth the proportion which each taxable person or corporation shall pay according to law.

SEC. 3. The city rate-bill maker shall be sworn to faithfully discharge the duties of his office, and said rate-bill maker and assessors shall receive such reasonable compensation as the Common Council shall allow.

SEC. 4. When said rate-bill shall have been made out, the Mayor of said city or one of the aldermen thereof, shall issue his warrant for the collection of the same, directed to the collector, commanding and empowering him to collect and pay the same to the City Treasurer within a time limited therein, which shall not be less than three months from the date of such warrant.

SEC. 5. The finance committee shall have power to abate the taxes of such persons in said city, as are poor and unable to pay the same.

CHAPTER XIX.

TRADE.

Be it ordained by the Common Council of the City of New Britain:

SECTION 1. No person shall vend upon the public streets of said city, any groceries, provisions, fruits, vegetables, or other merchandise, at any private or public sale or auction, unless such person shall have a license from the Common Council or the license committee thereof: *provided*, that this section shall not extend to sales by farmers, gardeners, and fish venders, of the products of the farms, gardens, and waters of this State; and any person offending against any provision of this section shall forfeit and pay a penalty of ten dollars for each offense.

SEC. 2. No person shall keep or have for sale, or any other purpose, in any house, store, or other building within the limits of said city, more than one pound of gunpowder, without previous license of the Common Council or the license committee thereof.

SEC. 3. No person licensed to keep or sell gunpowder pursuant hereto, shall have on hand at any one time more than fifty pounds in weight, and the same shall be kept in a chest of copper, tin, or some other incombustible material, marked on the front with the word "gunpowder," which chest shall have two stout handles, and a tight lid or cover with hinges, and no person shall sell any gunpowder except between sunrise and sunset.

SEC. 4. No person without license shall transport any gunpowder through said city or any street thereof, at any other time than between the rising and setting of the sun, nor in quantities of more than one hundred pounds at any one time, in any one vehicle, and only in accordance with the terms of the permission, which shall be first obtained of the Chief Engineer of the Fire Department of said city.

SEC. 5. Any person, offending against any of the provisions of the three preceding sections of this ordinance, shall forfeit and pay a penalty of not less than twenty nor more than one hundred dollars for each offense, and a like penalty for every day that such person shall have, keep, or possess any gunpowder contrary to the provisions of said sections.

SEC. 6. No person shall have, keep, or possess, or bring within the limits of said city any of the compound known as nitro-glycerine, and any person, so offending, shall forfeit and pay a penalty of one hundred dollars, and a like penalty for every day that such person shall have, keep, or possess any of said compound within said city.

SEC. 7. The license committee of the Common Council shall prescribe fees, (subject to appeal, by any party interested, to said Council,) for issuing licenses for any of the purposes aforesaid.

SEC. 8. There shall be appointed annually in the month of April by the Common Council a sealer of weights and measures, whose duty it shall be to annually inspect, prove correct, and seal all measures, scales, steelyards, and weights used for weighing or measuring by any person in doing business within said city, according to the standards of the city of New Britain. All such measures, scales, steelyards, and weights as are found, or made, to correspond and agree with said standards shall be marked or sealed with the letters N. B. S. In addition to said annual inspection said sealer of weights and measures shall, when requested by any person, try and test by said standards the measures, scales, steelyards, and weights used by any person doing business within said city.

SEC. 9. Any person who shall, within the limits of said city, use any weight or measure to ascertain the length, weight, or quantity of any article by him sold, which weight or measure has not been marked or sealed by said sealer of weights and measures in the manner provided in the eighth section of this ordinance, or who shall knowingly and with intent to defraud, sell any article as or for a greater weight, measure, or quantity than such article does in fact weigh or measure according to said standards, shall forfeit and pay a penalty of not less than two, nor more than twenty dollars.

SEC. 10. The owner of the several measures, scales, steelyards, and weights shall pay said sealer of weights and measures for each annual inspection made as required by section eight of this ordinance:—For testing each set of weights, twenty-five cents; set of measures from gill to gallon, twenty-five cents; each yardstick, five cents; set of measures, dry, twenty-five cents; for each scale, steelyard, balance, or basket, the sum of twenty-five cents each ; for each weight or measure less than a set, the sum of five cents each. When an additional inspection shall be made as provided in section eight of this ordinance, the expenses of such inspection shall be paid by the person requesting the same.

SEC. 11. The sealer of weights and measures shall visit from time to time, as he shall deem necessary, all places in said city where scales, weights, or measures of any kind are used in buying or selling any article of merchandise, and inspect such scales, weights, or measures, as have not been inspected within one year, and proceed as provided in section eight.

SEC. 12. It shall be the duty of the sealer of weights and measures, and it shall be lawful for him to enter any store, house, or any other building or yard in said city, where weights or measures are used for the purpose of buying or selling any article, at any reasonable hour, to inspect any scales, weights, or measures contained therein, and it shall be lawful for him to inspect the scales, weights, or measures of any itinerant merchant or peddler of fruits, vegetables, or other articles of merchandise in said city.

SEC. 13. It shall be the duty of every policeman to assist the sealer of weights and measures when required, and to report to him any violation within his knowledge, of any provisions of this ordinance relating to the use of weights and measures, and the sealer of weights and measures shall report the same to the city attorney for prosecution forthwith.

SEC. 14. Every person who shall hinder or obstruct said sealer of weights and measures in the discharge of the duties herein imposed upon him, shall forfeit and pay for each offense a penalty of ten dollars.

CHAPTER XX.

WATER.

Be it ordained by the Common Council of the City of New Britain:

SECTION 1. The Chairman of the Board of Water Commissioners shall be the Acting Commissioner, and to him the discharge of the active duties of the Board shall pertain, including the receipt and disbursement of all moneys and funds. Such Acting Commissioner shall receive, as compensation for his services, the sum of three dollars for each day of actual employment, and shall report monthly to the Common Council the number of days of actual employment during the previous month; and said sum per day shall also be received by each of the other Commissioners whenever his active services shall be required.

SEC. 2. It shall be the duty of the Water Commissioners to report, annually, to the Common Council, at its first meeting in April, a classified statement of all sums received by them from all sources, and all expenditures incurred by them, together with a general exhibit of the existing state of the water-works and the finances relating thereto, which report, having been duly audited, shall be recorded by the City Clerk and published in such manner as the Common Council shall direct. They shall also report at any time upon call of the Common Council.

SEC. 3. Each of the Water Commissioners shall give bond, with at least one sufficient surety for the faithful performance of his duty, the acting Commissioner in the sum of five thousand dollars, and the others in the sum of five hundred dollars each.

SEC. 4. Any person, who shall cause or allow water from the water-works of said city to be introduced upon premises owned or occupied by him, or who shall use an additional quantity of said water, or shall use it for a purpose different from that for which it has previously been used by him, without first obtaining the written consent of at least one of the Water Commissioners of said city, shall forfeit and pay for each offense a penalty of not less than five nor more than twenty dollars.

15

SEC. 5.   Any person who shall do the plumbing, or any part thereof, necessary to be done for the commission of any of the acts mentioned in section four, knowing that the consent therein required has not been obtained, shall be deemed guilty of a violation of this ordinance, and shall be subject to the penalty above named.

SEC. 6.   No owner or occupant of any premises shall allow any unnecessary waste of the public or "Shuttle Meadow" water; and whenever any such waste occurs, such owner or occupant shall forfeit and pay for each offense a penalty of not less than five nor more than twenty-five dollars.

CHAPTER XXI.

AN ORDINANCE TO CARRY INTO EFFECT THE REVISION OF THE ORDINANCES.

Be it ordained by the Common Council of the City of New Britain.

SECTION 1.   On and after the first day of January, 1877, the revision of the ordinances of said city, adopted November 1, 1876, as the same have been revised, arranged and incorporated together, and published under the supervision of, and by the committee on ordinances, in accordance with a resolution of the Common Council passed May 3, 1876, shall be and remain the ordinances of said city, and be entitled the Ordinances of the City of New Britain.

SEC. 2.   And whereas the ordinances of said city have heretofore, as they were passed, been published in a newspaper as required by the ordinance approved April 29, 1871, said revision shall be valid and operative without publication in any newspaper, notwithstanding said ordinance of April 29, 1871.

SEC. 3.   One copy of said ordinances as published by said committee on ordinances, shall be by them deposited, and thereafter kept, in the office of the City Clerk who shall annex thereto a certificate under his hand and the seal of said city, that the ordinances therein contained are the ordinances of said city, and such copy shall be an authentic record of such ordinances.

◆●◆

STANDING RULES OF THE COMMON COUNCIL OF THE CITY OF NEW BRITAIN.

I.   The Mayor, or in his absence, the Senior Alderman present, shall preside, and shall call the members to order, and upon the call of the roll and the appearance of a quorum, cause the records of the previous meeting to be read, that any mistakes in the same may be corrected.

II.   The business in order after reading of the records of the previous meeting, shall be, *first*, reception and disposal of petitions, and each petition and memorial shall be referred to a committee, unless the Council shall otherwise order ; *second*, reading and disposal of reports of committees, reports of standing committees to have preference ; *third*, unfinished business, including "orders of the day ; " *fourth*, new business ; *fifth*, adjournment.

III.   The presiding officer shall preserve order and decorum, may speak to questions of order in preference to other members, and shall decide questions of order, subject to appeal to the Council by any member.

IV.   Special committees shall be appointed by the presiding officer, unless otherwise specially directed ; and other committees may be chosen by nomination or resolution.

V.   Every petition, resolution or memorial, shall be offered by some member of the Council, who shall endorse thereon his name, and hand the same to the presiding officer before action by the Council.

VI.   When any member of the Council is about to speak, he shall rise from his seat, and respectfully address the presiding officer, shall confine himself to the question, and avoid personalities or imputing to any member improper motives ; and during debate, or when the presiding officer is speaking, no member shall hold private discourse, or pass between the speaker and the chair.

VII. If any member, in speaking or otherwise, transgress the rules of the Council, the chair shall, or any member may, call to order, in which case the member so called to order, shall sit down, unless permitted to explain. In case of an appeal to the Council, and a decision in favor of the member called to order, he shall be at liberty to proceed ; otherwise, he shall not be permitted to proceed without leave of the Council.

VIII. When a motion is made and seconded, it shall be stated by the presiding officer, or being in writing, shall be read aloud before being debated ; every motion shall be reduced to writing, at the request of the chair, or any member.

IX. No member shall speak more than twice on the same question, without leave of the Council, unless to explain.

X. When a motion is stated by the presiding officer, it shall be deemed to be in possession of the Council, but may be withdrawn at any time before decision or amendment, but not after amendment, unless the Council give leave, and when a motion has been carried, it shall be in order for any member in the majority to move the reconsideration thereof, within two meetings after the one at which such motion was carried, and such motion shall take precedence of all questions, except a motion to adjourn.

XI. When a question is under debate, no motion shall be received but to adjourn, to lay on the table, to postpone to a day certain, to commit or amend, or to postpone indefinitely ; which several motions shall have precedence in the order in which they stand arranged. The motion to adjourn shall always be in order, that, and the motion to lay on the table, shall be decided without debate.

XII. The yeas and nays shall be taken when called for by any member, and when taken, the names of the members shall be called in the order of wards.

XIII. No member shall be excused from voting on any question, unless he is personally interested in the result, or shall be excused by a vote of the Council, and no member shall be permitted to vote after the decision is announced by the presiding officer.

XIV. No rules shall be suspended, except by a vote of two-thirds of the members present.

AMENDMENTS TO THE ORDINANCES.

PASSED BY THE COMMON COUNCIL PREVIOUS TO JULY 1, 1881.

DOGS.

AN ORDINANCE IN ALTERATION OF AN ORDINANCE ENTITLED " DOGS."

Be it ordained by the Common Council of the City of New Britain:

That Section 2 of Chapter V, of the ordinance entitled Dogs be amended by striking out the words "between the first day of July and the first day of October in any year."

FIRE.

AN ORDINANCE IN ALTERATION OF AN ORDINANCE ENTITLED " FIRE."

Be it ordained by the Common Council of the City of New Britain:

SECTION 1. From and after July 1, 1881, Hose Company Nos. 1 and 3 shall consist of ten men, and Hose Company No. 2 shall consist of eight men.

NUISANCE.

AN ORDINANCE IN ALTERATION OF AN ORDINANCE ENTITLED " NUISANCE."

Be it ordained by the Common Council of the City of New Britain:

That Chapter XI, Section 1 of the ordinances concerning Nuisances be amended by inserting after the word "City" in the 44th line, the following words, to wit:

Or reassembling in like manner with the same or other persons upon the same day or evening after having been so commanded to disperse.

AN ORDINANCE IN ALTERATION OF AN ORDINANCE ENTITLED " NUISANCE."

Be it ordained by the Common Council of the City of New Britain:

SECTION 1. The ordinance of said city concerning " Nuisance," being Chapter XI of the City Ordinance, is hereby amended by striking out the whole of Section 4 in said chapter, and inserting in lieu thereof the following :

SEC. 4. No person, without the consent of the Health committee, shall build or maintain any privy or cess-pool in said city, within forty feet of any well, or twenty-five feet of any street line, dwelling house, shop, factory, or public building, nor without leaving at least two feet of solid earth or mason work laid in cement between such privy or cess-pool and the lot adjoining.

POLICE.

AN ORDINANCE IN ALTERATION OF AN ORDINANCE ENTITLED " POLICE."

Be it ordained by the Common Council of the City of New Britain :

That Section 10 of Chapter XIII of the city ordinances be, and the same is hereby amended so as to read as follows :

Any Policeman who shall act as Constable of the town of New Britain, or who shall act as any other officer of said town in any capacity in which he is entitled to receive salary, fees, or emoluments, or who shall engage in any business interfering at all with his duties as Policemen, shall be deemed to have tendered his resignation as Policeman, and the same shall be accepted by the Common Council, and his place as Policeman be filled or declared vacant.

PUBLIC CONVEYANCES.

Resolved.—That the ordinance relative to Public Conveyances so much of Section 4 as relates to funerals and weddings, be changed to read as follows:

For going to and from funerals, two dollars; and for attending weddings, three dollars.

AN ORDINANCE AMENDING THE ORDINANCE RELATIVE TO " PUBLIC CONVEYANCES."

Be it ordained by the Common Council of the City of New Britain :

SECTION 1. That Chapter XIV of the Ordinances of said city, being an ordinance concerning Public Conveyances, be amended as follows :

By striking out in Section 2 of said ordinance all after the word "city " in the second line of said section and before the word "unless" in the fifth line of the same section, so that said section shall read: "No public carriage shall be used within the limits of said city, unless the same shall be duly licensed by the Chief of Police, and every such license shall be in writing and expire on the first Monday of May succeeding its date, and shall be recorded before being issued by said Chief of Police, in a book kept for the purpose ;" and by striking out in Section 3 of said Ordinance the words "or other vehicles" in the first line of said section.

SALARIES AND BONDS.

AN ORDINANCE IN ALTERATION OF AN ORDINANCE ENTITLED "SALARIES AND BONDS."

Be it ordained by the Common Council of the City of New Britain :

That Section 1 of Chapter XV of the ordinances entitled Salaries and Bonds be amended by striking out the words "two per cent. on the amount of taxes collected," and inserting in their place the words, "one per cent. on the amount paid into the Treasury of taxes on which a discount of five per cent. is made, and three and one-half per cent. on the remainder of the taxes collected, and one per cent. on the amount of Street, Sewer, and Stream assessments collected."

AN ORDINANCE IN ALTERATION OF AN ORDINANCE ENTITLED "SALARIES AND BONDS."

Be it ordained by the Common Council of the City of New Britain :

That Section 1, Chapter XV, of the Ordinances entitled "Salaries and Bonds," be amended by striking out the words "of five per cent." and by substituting in place of the words, "three and one-half per cent. on the remainder of the taxes collected," the words "one and one-half per cent. on the amount of taxes collected on which no discount is made."

AN ORDINANCE IN ALTERATION OF AN ORDINANCE ENTITLED "SALARIES AND BONDS."

Be it ordained by the Common Council of the City of New Britain :

The city Ordinance concerning Salaries and Bonds as contained in Chapter XV of the city ordinances is hereby amended by striking out the word "five" in the second line of Section five of said

Chapter, and inserting in lieu thereof the word "fifteen," and by striking out the word "three" in the third line of said Section and inserting in lieu thereof the word "five."

SEWERS.

An Ordinance in alteration of an Ordinance relative to "Sewers."

Be it ordained by the Common Council of the City of New Britain:

That Chapter XVI of the Ordinances of said city, being an Ordinance concerning Sewers, be and the same is hereby amended by striking out the whole of Section 5 of said ordinance, and enacting in lieu thereof the following:

Sec. 5. No person or corporation shall allow steam from the premises owned and occupied by them to enter any public sewer, nor shall they without the consent of the Common Council first obtained, allow air to be forced from such premises into any sewer, by means of a blower or otherwise, and any person offending against the provisions of this Section, shall forfeit and pay to the city a penalty of fifty dollars for each offense, and each week's continued violation shall constitute a separate offense.

WATER.

An Ordinance in addition to an Ordinance entitled "Water."

Be it ordained by the Common Council of the City of New Britain:

Sec. 7. The Water Commissioners may cause the water of the Water Works of said City to be shut off from the premises of any person or corporation neglecting or refusing to pay rent for the use of said water within the time limited for the payment thereof in the rules and regulations adopted by said Commissioners for said Water Works, or for the willful neglect or violation of any of said rules and regulations; and any person, who, without the written consent of at least one of said Commissioners, shall again let on said water on the premises of the person or corporation so neglecting or offending, shall forfeit and pay a penalty of not less than five nor more than twenty dollars for each offense.

CITY AUDITOR.

AN ORDINANCE CONCERNING THE DUTIES OF THE CITY AUDITOR.

Be it ordained by the Common Council of the City of New Britain:

SECTION 1.   It shall be the duty of the City Auditor, in auditing the accounts of the City Collector, to ascertain the amount of taxes uncollected and due the city on each and every city rate bill, and also the amounts due the city on all warrants for the collection of assessments on account of public improvements of all kinds, and to report the same to the Common Council.

THE PUBLIC PARK.

AN ORDINANCE CONCERNING THE PUBLIC PARK.

Be it ordained by the Common Council of the City of New Britain:

SECTION 1.   No person shall trample upon the grass or grounds outside of the regular walks in the public Park of the city opposite the Center Church, or injure any of the trees, plants, flowers, or shrubbery thereon, or commit any nuisance in or about said park.

SEC. 2.   Any person who shall violate the provisions of this ordinance shall forfeit and pay a penalty of not less than one nor more than twenty dollars for each offense.

FIRE ALARM TELEGRAPH.

AN ORDINANCE IN REFERENCE TO THE FIRE ALARM TELEGRAPH.

Be it ordained by the Common Council of the City of New Britain:

SECTION 1.   No person shall post or in any manner affix any placards, bills, or notice, either written or printed, upon any of the Fire Alarm Telegraph poles or boxes in said city.

SEC. 2.   No person shall hitch or fasten any horse or other animal to any of the Fire Alarm Telegraph poles is said city.

SEC. 3.   No person shall willfully injure, deface, or in any manner interfere with any of the Fire Alarm Telegraph poles, boxes, wires, or any of the apparatus connected with the Fire Alarm Telegraph.

SEC. 4.   Any person offending against any of the provisions of this ordinance, shall forfeit and pay for each offense a penalty of not less than five nor more than twenty-five dollars.

AMENDMENTS TO THE CITY CHARTER.

AN ACT IN ADDITION TO AN ACT INCORPORATING THE CITY OF NEW BRITAIN.

Be it enacted by the Senate and House of Representatives in General Assembly convened:

SECTION 1. Whenever any of the members of the Board of Street Commissioners of said city shall be disqualified, by interest or otherwise, from acting in any case before said board, the mayor of said city, by and with the advice of any two of the aldermen of said city, may appoint one or more disinterested freeholders of said city to fill the places of the members so disqualified, and such persons having been sworn by the clerk of said city to a faithful and impartial discharge of their duties, and a certificate of such appointment and the administration of such oaths having been recorded in the records of said city, all the procedings before said board shall be as now provided in the charter of said city and the amendments thereof.

SEC. 2. The persons appointed in accordance with the preceding section shall receive the same compensation as the regular members of said board, but they shall act only in the cases for which they were appointed, and in all other cases the regular members of said board shall act as before.

SEC. 3. This act shall take effect from and after its passage.

Approved, March 26, 1878.

AN ACT AMENDING THE CHARTER OF THE CITY OF NEW BRITAIN.

Be it enacted by the Senate and House of Representatives in General Assembly convened:

SECTION 1. That an Act incorporating the city of New Britain, passed by the General Assembly of this State at the May session thereof, A.D. 1870, and approved July 15, 1870, be amended by adding after the word "the," and before the word "absence" in the third line of section fifteen, the word "death."

SEC. 2. In all cases where liens are created by said Act incorporating the city of New Britain, or by the acts amendatory thereof or in additions thereto, on account of public improvements of any kind in said city, such liens shall, if an appeal shall be taken from the appraisal of damages or assessment of benefits, or both, continue to exist for a period of sixty days after the passage of the final decree of the court or judge having jurisdiction of such appeal, or after termination of the appeal proceedings, but not longer, unless within such time a certificate signed by the mayor of said city or the clerk of the common council thereof, describing the premises on which such lien exists, and the amount claimed by said city as a lien thereon, shall be lodged with the clerk of the town of New Britain.

SEC. 3. This act shall be a public act, and shall take effect from its passage, and all acts inconsistent herewith are hereby repealed.

Approved, March 19, 1879.

INDEX.

INDEX.

A.

C.

D.

E.

F.

G.

H.

P.

www.ingramcontent.com/pod-product-compliance
Lightning Source LLC
Chambersburg PA
CBHW030600270326
41927CB00007B/988